BEFORE YOU GO

Joe Holman

I joyfully dedicate this book to my role model and mentor, the mother of my 11 children, Denise.

You teach us by your example. I am so blessed to call you my wife. As I always say about the kids, "I break them, you fix them." I am so happy you are even better at fixing than I am at breaking!

WHY LISTEN TO ME?

What kind of father would let his 19-year-old son spend his first Thanksgiving Holiday from home alone in another city, sleeping in a car in a Walmart parking lot? Especially when you know the son was not, as the saying goes, "learning life lessons from hitting bottom". Here is a young man living for Jesus, attending a Christian university, working three jobs, and enrolled in ROTC in order to enlist in the Army as an Officer. He doesn't drink. He doesn't use any form of drugs. He has no obvious and known sin in his life. Yet, he spent his first ever holiday away from us as a homeless man. He slept in the passenger seat of a 20-year-old Chevy sedan.

Probably the same type of dad that would put his 18-year-old son on a plane and send him off to another continent without a job, home, car or money. This is the same father who waved as his oldest son walked up the stairway of the plane on the tarmac, not to see him again for two years.

This is the man writing a book on how to send your children off as adults? This man teaches how we need to prepare our children for the world before they leave our homes? It sounds like you may have wasted your money on buying this book. Seriously, what could I tell you about releasing your adult children? It is like a prostitute giving a conference on chastity or a gangster talking about ethics. An author is supposed to either be an expert, or have done a lot of research in the field before writing a book.

I am not an expert. However, I did and am still doing a lot of field research in the topic of parenting. I guess you could say that I have lived in a laboratory for over 30 years. In the last thirty years, we have:

- Changed over 42,000 diapers.
- Prepared 192,680 plates.
- Had preschoolers for 25 years.
- Had teenagers for 19 years (We have 8 more years to go...we will have had teenagers for 27 years when finished)
- Have experienced seven children leaving the nest to live on their own. Two more will leave us this year.
- Five married children with one more to wed in November of this year.

How is that possible? We have eleven children. Not that big of a deal, because the most we have had at home at the same time was only 10 (for 12 years). To understand the math, if we have 10 children at home, then my wife prepares 36 meals per day (10 kids, 2 parents, 3 meals). That is 13,140 per year. That is how the numbers add up. We had children in diapers for over 23 years.

Yes, we have eleven children. Yes, we own a tv and we know what causes it. No, we are not Catholics, Mormons or on welfare. We have 11 children because we truly believe that children are a blessing. We strive to pour our lives into them. We choose to homeschool them, not because of a fear of public school or some whacked out reason. We want to be with them as much as possible. My wife gave up a full scholarship in mathematics and left the workplace in order to be a stay-at-home mom.

Yet, it is hard to fight the feeling of failure.

Did we do enough?

Should we have done this or maybe tried that? Are they ready for life?

How badly did we mess them up?

We planned on being there when our children grew up and left our home. We actually worked it out in our minds. They would do their last two years of high school in a dual enrollment program with our local community college. They would have two years of college before they graduated high school. Then, they would live at home and work a gap year in order to save up money. After that, attend a university near our home, allowing them to live at home and save money. Once they graduated from university, they would begin their career as close to family as possible. We established the plan together with them.

School and work were not the only thing. We had their future marriage partners all planned out as well. Not really 'planned'. It wasn't like we had a list of hair color and skill sets that they had to produce before dating. Our plan was to be a part, a huge part, of their lives and relationships. Since we were such a part, then naturally when it came to dating and finding a spouse, we would be there. We never were part of the 'courtship', and/or 'arranged marriage' subculture. However, we intended to be a part of their journey when they found a potential spouse. We would have them over to our home. We would get to know their family. We would do events together. We would be with them relationally from first date to last child.

Then God changed it all.

In 2007, my wife and I answered God's call to leave our home and pastorate in Loudoun County, Virginia. He called us from the wealthiest county in the United States to serve Him in the poorest country in all the Americas. We packed up and headed to Cochabamba, Bolivia. We have been there ever since.

God messed up my entire parenting plan. He not only messed up what I had planned, He made it impossible to accomplish my plans. So, when you hear of how our kids left home, it sounds like we are horrible parents. Instead of a smooth transition from their junior year in high school through college, our first son left home with mom and dad crying in a two-gate airport in the Andes Mountains. He headed off to another continent to start his life as an adult with no money, no car, no house, and no job. He left to go live with grandparents for a few months before he could get on his own. We could not fly to the States with him because our passports were tied up in the country's visa office. In place of visiting us on holidays and long weekends, my third son spent his very first Thanksgiving on his own living in his car. He attended a small college and unknown to us or him, the school shut the dorms down completely over the holidays. No exceptions. My son worked three jobs and could not afford to quit them. He was prohibited from visiting relatives because of his jobs. He ate a hamburger in a parking lot for his Thanksgiving meal and slept in his car for two weeks. This broke my wife's heart. Can you imagine this as a parent? We could not visit or afford to pay for him to stay in a hotel. He was paying his own way through school and did not have the extra cash for a hotel. He is an introvert and had not yet made friends. So, my 19-year-old son was homeless and alone on his first Thanksgiving. It was not because of sin. It was because all of us were in the will of God.

What happened when my first son left shook up our world. We had not yet worked through how to 'release our arrows' in this new environment. The plan was for our 18-year-old son to live with us for three years and then return to the States. However, after a few months, he decided to get on with his life. That meant leaving us. We did not have time to prepare. His lived with his grandparents until he could step out on his own. After moving out, his first two roommates were from Craigslist. We realized something. God changed our original plans, and we did not replace them with new ones. We needed to help with the transition from child to adult, from home to alone. We could not be there in person. We could give guidance and advice before they left.

The Bible says children are like arrows in the hands of a warrior (Psalms 127). The purpose of an arrow is to fly from the bow towards a target. The archer chooses and aims at the target. We wanted to release our arrows so when our children struck adulthood, they would bring glory to God by who they were and what they did. We knew we could no longer be there for them. Therefore, my wife and I wrote an unpublished personal book for each child. I call it *"Before You Go"*. We took time to think about the things we wanted our adults, not our children, but our adults to know. The year before our children leave home, we give them this book. We meet each week for one or two hours to talk about the contents. It is not a Bible study. It includes basic life stuff you can easily find Bible passages to reinforce. The book is advice. It comprises actions and attitudes to help them enjoy and be successful at life.

I decided to rewrite the book and publish it. I thought, in the age of self-publication, it could be a great legacy for them and their children. My goal expanded, and I decided to make our personal book available for parents. If it serves no other purpose but to help you think through what you really want your adult children to know, and then develop some form of communicating it to them, then this book is successful.

Allow me to give you two qualifiers.

First, we are evangelical Christians and all of my children have committed their lives to Christ and follow Him. That base and foundation is covered, so there are no chapters on repentance and how to be saved. They all know this is the most important thing in all eternity, not just to be successful in life.

The second one is I wrote this book for my children. I am publishing it, but I wrote it for them. It might have grammatical errors. I tweak it for each child and make it personal, but this is for them. I will also reference our lives together as a family. I will do this multiple times. The entire point of the book was to let my children, and hopefully multiple generations, look at how we have followed Christ and Biblical principles in our lives so they can do the same in theirs.

THE SECRET OF LIFE

Remember the house we lived in up on the hill? It had a secret hiding place. We opened the kitchen cabinet to put up our pans, and I noticed the bottom was a piece of plywood. I moved it and we discovered it was a trapdoor. Below the kitchen was a hidden concrete bunker. It was seven feet high, and ten by ten wide. The only entrance or exit was the trapdoor under the pans in the kitchen. One of your friends came over and you guys all played hide and seek. I let you crawl into the bunker and put the pans back. She looked for twenty minutes and could not find you. Several times, she walked through the kitchen, literally six inches above you. We showed the place to her. You guys made it into your own little playroom and secret headquarters. I wonder how many people rented the house before, and after us, without knowing the secret bunker was there. I wonder why the original builder of the home put it there. Whatever the reason, the house had a secret place under the kitchen. A room unknown to most people.

I want to share with you the secret of life. It is just like that little room. People walk past it. It is there, waiting for them. We just don't really enter it. The illustration breaks down because this secret is not a secret. It is broadcast. It is stated. Jesus proclaimed it. It goes from the Old Testament through the New Testament. It is literally one of the major themes of Scripture. I call it a secret because so few people live it. It is the path to a joyful life. It is the means to a fruitful life. It is the way to a meaningful life. We walk right past it with blindfolds on our faces. It is there, we just do not see it.

It is not a secret.

Jesus said it was the most important thing we could do. Here is it: Love God With All Your Heart, Mind, Soul, And Strength.

I bet you did not see this one coming as the first thing, did you? :) You heard this your entire life. Love God. You know my life mission statement. You heard it in my messages, teaching and normal conversation. The purpose of my life is "Helping people know God better and love Him more." 1 Timothy states the goal of our instruction is love. It is all about your love for Him. Your love and relationship with him is the center of your life. Everything else is a spoke branching off the center. If He, and your love for Him, is not the centerpiece, your entire life is out of balance. Love God with all you are, and you will have joy. Love God with all you are, and you will bear fruit. Love God with all you are, and your life takes purpose and meaning. Love God with all you are, and your relationships fall into place. We respond to His love at the cross. We love Him because He first loved us. It is all about loving God. We taught you the importance of a quiet time. A devotional is not the same as loving God. God is way more concerned with your passion, focus, and your desire towards Him than He is with whether you read five verses this morning. Never let the disciplines become a substitute for love. Love God. Really love Him. Put Him first—in front of you and all other people and things—always and every day. He is the reason for your existence. He is the Author and Finisher of your faith, your life, your all.

How can you love Him? The first key is by believing, with faith more real than sight, that God loves you. Rest in His love. I will talk about this in another chapter. Just remember, constantly, He loves you!

Second, your love and passion grow as you worship the Lord. Remember the times we spent in prayer together, and how mom and I would worship Christ as we stated His Names and attributes? You saw us singing, dancing, and verbally praising Him. The Bible tells us to shout, praise, express our joy and declare His Name. We raise our hands in worship, both privately and publicly. This engages our emotions. Worship of God is not just acknowledging His worth. It is feeling it. Worship God. Be excited. Think about Who you are in the Presence of, and what it means to be there. God in all of His Glory is with you! When you are in church, don't sing like a robot, sing TO God. Imagine you are in front of the throne, singing directly to Him. He receives your worship with a glad heart. I rewrite the lyrics to fit a first-person expression. The lyrics might say, "We worship You". I sing, "I worship You." Raise your hands, close your eyes, bend your knees...He is the God of all Creation and He Loves YOU. Love Him back.

Love Him with your mind as well. Our culture likes to focus on the physical yet ignore the intellectual. I once read somewhere 75% of people never read a book after finishing high school. God gave us our minds for us to think. Think about Him. Read theology and philosophy. Memorize Scripture. Listen to podcasts and Bible studies. Examine opposing viewpoints to your current beliefs about the fringe doctrines. Listen to what others have to say. Think about Scripture. Seek to grow in wisdom, knowledge, understanding, and insight. We need to not just have faith, but to have intelligent faith. Stretch your mind and add to its capacity. Give your intellect to Him and grow. Think about your life up to this point. every day, you witnessed us reading books to learn. Mom is the Empress of Research. We watch documentaries. We take courses. We do what we can to understand God and how to better live out our faith.

As you love Him, you will want to spend time with Him. This is where the strength...or effort part comes in. Make it a priority to talk to Him and hear from Him each day. I do this in two parts (the second is more important). First, have the traditional quiet time heard about all your life. Start your day off with an extended time of worship, the word, and prayer. You must make this a priority, or it will not happen. I believe this is the most important part of the entire day...if anything or everything else must go, then let it go. Musicians tune their instrument before the concert. Athletes stretch before the game. Maintenance is always proactive. A quiet time each day is all of these and more. It is preparing your heart and mind to be in tune with Christ before your day starts. We can be like Christ in the world if we are with Christ on our own.

Not only have the private time with God, but all day long give yourself to Him (I will talk about this more in the Abiding section). We have made a mistake in evangelical Christianity. We believe giving God some of our time in the morning is the same thing as giving Him our lives. God doesn't want some time, He deserves and desires all the time. Constantly focus on the Lord. This is love. Be with Him. Talk to Him. Listen to Him, Think about Him. He is everything. Love God.

DO THE CREED

I just arrived from the airport with a short-term team. You and I wait for them to rest before our first team meeting. Quick question for you. What do I talk about at the first meeting with a new team? You saw and heard it so many times. One of you made a construction paper and crayon rendition of the first four. We hung it by the kitchen. I take it down off the wall and use it with the team to teach them. You have it memorized. It is our family creed.

No Whiner Babies.
Apply The Stupid Rule.
Don't Be A Jerk.
Honor Christ In All You Do.
Be Kind To Everyone.
Always Tell The Truth.
Forgive Instantly.
Believe The Bible.

Those eight little nuggets gave us some simple guidelines for life together. I will expand on some of them in other chapters. Let me talk here about the ones I won't devote a chapter to explain.

No Whiner Babies. We stressed this with our short-term teams. We lived it out in our lives. From the time you were a baby, we did not allow whining. You might remember the timer we used on your little siblings. We used it on you as well, but you were so young you don't remember it. If you whined in any form, we stopped you. "I don't speak whiner baby." We said. I set a timer for sixty seconds. "You stop and think how to say what you want in English, with no whining. In a minute you can try again." We instructed you. If you whined the next time, we repeated the process until you stopped whining. You learned to not whine.

Adults don't whine like children. In adults we see whining in complaining and murmuring. We did not allow you to complain. Typically, if one of you complained about a task, we assigned more of that task. I know you can hear my voice say, "If you cannot handle a 'No', you will never hear a 'Yes'." Complaining and murmuring are normal in our culture. Don't do it. Sometimes life is unfair. You do not get the results you expected. Others receive a break. People do not meet your expectations. Your boss is not nice. Someone assigns you a job or task you do not want or like. Over and over it goes. These give us many opportunities to whine and complain. Don't do it. Suck it up and do a heart-check. Repent of your attitude and receive joy instead. Anyone can have a great attitude doing what they want to do. You reveal your character by having a great attitude doing what you do not want to do. Do not whine, solve the problem. Do not whine, do the job. Do not whine, meet your responsibility.

Apply The Stupid Rule. You follow this rule and I cannot tell you how much pain you will avoid. It is simple and easy to do. If your friends or someone tries to get you to do something, or f something tempts you, ask yourself: Would a stupid person do this? Is this a stupid thing? If the answer to either of those questions is yes, don't do it. You know what you call someone who does stupid things? Stupid. Stupid is as stupid does. Don't be stupid with your money, time, talent, or relationships. Don't take stupid chances. Don't say stupid things. Apply the Stupid Rule. Don't be stupid.

Don't be a jerk. You know, we sometimes used stronger language to describe this one. We find the beauty of these life rules in their simplicity. Here are a few synonyms for jerk: idiot, fool, rascal, brute, blockhead, dolt, dunce, imbecile. You can put any of those words into our creed. Don't be an idiot. Don't be a fool. Don't be a blockhead. Don't be a dolt.

Don't be a jerk. I know more than a few Christians who are

jerks. They think folks dislike them because of their faith in Christ. They call the disdain of others some form of persecution. I want to tell them, "People don't like you because you are obnoxious, mean, judgmental, pushy, rude, arrogant, and harsh. It isn't Jesus or Christianity they dislike. It is you. That is because you are a jerk." I don't say it, but want I want to tell them. Kiddo, do not be a jerk. Treat others with kindness and respect. Gracefully disagree if expressing your opinion or a Biblical truth. Don't be defensive or aggressive. If you talk to a person who has a different political viewpoint, don't be a jerk. If someone does something you did not want them to do. Don't be a jerk. If people do not meet your expectations, don't be a jerk. Help and bless others. It is all found in that little phrase: Don't be a jerk.

REST IN GOD'S LOVE

If I say the phrase, "Sunday afternoon", what image comes to your mind? I bet it is our nap. Mom and I always take a nap on Sunday afternoon. Preaching wears me out. What do you think of when you remember our family vacations? Give me a one-word response. I know you said "Beach", or "Cruise". Go one thought deeper. What did we do a lot of when on our vacations? We relaxed. We rested. We never took vacations packed full of activity. We read a lot of books. We chilled in the sun and breeze. We played cards, dominoes, and board games. We did paint by number projects. We slept a lot. Our vacations are times of rest. We sought to instill within you growing up an understanding of the importance of rest. Mom and I try to get nine hours of sleep a night. This is counterculture in the good old USA. People run on fumes. People breakdown and are stressed out. We chose to rest, not stress. I take Saturdays and Mondays off work. I do not answer my phone or emails on those days. We unplug completely. This is because it is vital to our lives. God designed it that way. We need rest.

Rest means you stop expending effort. You do not work. You stop trying to do something. We need to rest in God's love. Stop expending effort to get Him to love you. Don't try to earn His love. Instead, rest in it.

We love God in response to His love for us. He loves us. You need to rest in His love. Many times people say things like, "I can't love myself." Low self-esteem is a buzzword. Here is the deal. You do not need to esteem yourself, if you rest in His estimation of you. He loves you. Just rest in it. Understand how much He loves you.

He loves you in the same way that He loves His Son. He loves you unconditionally. His love for you will never and has never changed. We cannot understand it. We believe it. He loves you with an everlasting love from eternity to eternity. He loved you before He created the world. He loves you now and he will love you forever. He does not love you because of what you do for Him or to Him. He loves you because He is love and He chose to love you. His love is proactive, not reactive. His love does not respond to us. We respond to it.

Many times we evaluate the love of God upon us by our circumstances. If things are good, then God loves us. We think the opposite to be true; if times are not good then God is mad at us. This is a lie from the enemy. God doesn't prove His love for us by what He does for us each day. He proved it in Jesus Christ and His death on the cross for us. The cross proves He loves us with an eternal love. He doesn't prove that He loves you by giving you the job, the girl, the car, or your health. Remember when Seth died? Before He died, we were praying for Him to recover. I said, "God will not prove His love by my son living, He proved His love by His Son dying." That is an eternal truth for you to anchor your life. It is proved. That is past tense. He proved He loves you by giving His Son.

I like to use economics to illustrate this truth. We studied economics, price, demand, supply, scarcity, and all of that. Scarcity, along with need, supply and demand of something determines value. God is omnipotent. God is perfect. God is unchanging. He can do anything and nothing diminishes His power or Who He is. He can create a multiverse with the same effort as he takes to create a grain of sand. Everything is in unlimited supply to Him. There is no such thing as a precious commodity. A diamond has the same value as a cow's patty. Think about it. He paved the streets of Heaven with gold and the gates are gemstones. God created the universe and all in it with a word. Everything in and out of all creation is unlimited to Him. The only thing in limited supply to God is Himself. He is the only uncreated. Let that sink in. The only thing in limited supply to God is God. That is the price He paid for you!

He gave the only thing that cost Him anything and it cost Him everything.

Remember, God gave the only thing that cost Him anything and it cost Him everything. His Son is eternal, uncreated, one of a Kind and irreplaceable. He paid the price of His Son for you. He offered the precious blood of the lamb, His Son. That is how much He loves you! Rest in that love. Trust it. Believe it.

LOVE OTHERS

I attend a lot of conferences. At the conference registration table, you pick up your name badge. The name badge identifies you as both a paid attendee and also as a means of introduction to other. People can see you belong and who you are. Our church has "Name Tag Sunday" once a month. All of us put a name tag on our shirts in order to meet others. A name badge is the way people identify you.

Every week, whether in Bolivia or the States, we show our identification to someone. In Bolivia it is our Carnet. In the States, it is our license. We show it to others in order to let them see who we are. It identifies us. What is the name badge, the identification tag, of a Christian? Love is our name badge that identifies us as His Children.

Short-term teams always purchase Bolivianitas. It is the semiprecious gem found only in Bolivia. I like the manner they display it at the jewelry shop. The jeweler places them on a black felt background and shines a bright light on them. The dark background showcases their refracting and color. Our love for others should be like this. We shine best when the world does not. We love amid hate.

How do we do that?

What is love?

We misunderstand love. Mercy was five years old when she coined the term, "Crappaccino". She asked mom one morning in her cute little voice, "Mommy, want me to get you a Crappaccino?" That was seven years ago, and we still call them crappuccinos. She changed the word. People changed the word love. It is a pit you might accidentally stumble and "fall in love". It is also a ledge where one might "fall out of love". It happens at "first sight". It might be we "slowly came to love each other". It is sex if you are "making love". It is an emotion. It seems to be something we cannot control. It is universal. You love God, french fries and Marvel. People in church speak about love as if it is a simple decision. You "choose to love". Christians are almost stoic in their view of love. A great refrigerator magnet is this one: "Love is a verb".

I hope that last paragraph helped you. Do you understand what love is now?

Our family, friends, co-workers and neighbors need to look at us and see Love. Our official identification is love. It is the only weapon that we have to defeat the enemy of our souls. We are to love others. But no can answer the simple question, "What is love?".

I know you heard me teach on this, but it is so important I want to do it again, to put you in remembrance. 1 Corinthians teaches that love is to be our priority (13:1-4). All that we do, if we do not do it in love, adds up to nothing. Our spiritual gifts, our wisdom, and our sacrifices are meaningless if we do not have love. Love is the Greatest Commandment according to Jesus, and it is to be the priority of our lives.

We see a description of love in verses 4-8. Therefore, people say "Love is a verb". Love produces change in our lives. I think we misinterpret these verses. These verses and descriptions are not a 'to-do' list. God is not telling us when we are patient, then we are loving. This is not a task list of assignments. I believe it is a checklist. I can look at this passage and see if I am indeed loving because if I am, these things are in my life. I know I love you because I am patient with you. If I am not patient, at that moment I am do not love you. Look at your life, your fruit, and see if reveals a loving heart. If not, then go to the cross for forgiveness and power. I do not get love by being kind. I see my love by my kindness. I also see the lack of love through being unkind. These character qualities reveal the presence or absence of love. God's love in my life changes me and those changes are visible. I love people in the manner God does, unconditionally.

Love is a verb. That is true, but only in part. Love is a multi-faceted and complex thing. I believe we are incapable of manu-facturing, or creating, this type of love. We cannot love people without conditions. We want to be the type of person the Bible describes, but we simply cannot love our enemy the same way that we love our friend. We cannot love anyone unconditionally. Yet, God tells us to. More than that, He commands us to. So, whazzup? We are incapable of creating this type of love, but not incapable of having or giving it. This is because love is a fruit. Love is not something that I do, it is something that I receive. Love is a fruit of the Holy Spirit, not a work of the flesh. This means, that in order for me to have the love of God, the Holy Spirit must give it to me. He will do this as I am filled with the Spirit and allow Him to control me. The best way to illustrate this is the good ole UPS man. When I order something, say a 500 gig external drive from Amazon, the UPS guy delivers it. He doesn't pull up in my driveway and break out a manual and a soldering iron, and make the thumb drive. The UPS guy is not in the business of manufacturing. He is a delivery man. He looks at the address on the box and delivers the item to me. We do the same with love. God loves the people in your life. He wants them to experience His love. So, He gives you His love in the fruit of the Holy Spirit, and you are to deliver, not manufacture, but deliver His love to them. This goes back to the first thing. In order to love others, I must love God.

This is the last thing about love. Love is not something I do, it is something I receive. Love is not only something that I receive; it is someone that I am with. The Bible teaches God is love. Love is a person. God Himself is love. He told us this in 1 John. Twice it says God is love. Love is a Person!

I love God. I spend time with the Person of God. As I am with Him and grow to be like Him, the Person of love gives me the product of love. He produces the spiritual fruit of love in my life. This love changes me and helps me become like Christ. The more I am like Jesus, the more of His Love I receive and the more of His love I give to others, to people He loves. The Person of

Love delivers the Product of His love through me.

Learn to love, really love, others. This makes life worth living and you like God.

BELIEVE THE BIBLE

What do you believe?

Who do you believe?

Why do you believe it?

These are serious questions. In recent years we have seen how these apply to life. President Trump coined the term, "Fake News". People ran with it. We do not believe news reported by those who differ from us. We do not look at the facts if the other side presented them. We do not believe them, therefore we do not believe their facts. "Fake News" describes all news other than what I want to believe. My faith in my side, and my lack of faith in the other, determines what I believe. Who I believe decides what I believe?

I share Christ a lot. I discovered in sharing my faith the importance of the root of our faith. Someone will tell me they do not believe in Christ. They tell me their belief. I can ask, "Why do you believe that?" I ask derivatives of this question, in a loving non-confrontational manner, to take them to their final faith. Everyone starts life off by faith. There is no conflict between faith and knowledge. Faith precedes knowledge. Without faith, we cannot know anything.

Let me illustrate this. I spoke with an atheist. He had a Ph.D. in Biology. I asked him what he believed. He talked about evolution and science. He said, "If we cannot empirically verify it, I do not believe it."

I wrote this sentence. "I only believe what we empirically verify." I asked him if this described him. He said it did, so I followed up with this question: "Did you empirically verify that sentence? What type of experimentation did you use to prove you can use experiments?" We talked for a while. He finally admitted his belief in naturalism and the philosophy of science was a faith. He believed the empirical method could deliver truth before he used the empirical method to discover truth.

How do you know what you know? There are limited avenues to gaining knowledge. The empirical method is one. I gain knowledge through my five senses. Logic is another means. I can deduce or induce from information. We build the discipline of mathematics on logic. If this is true, then we can deduce/induce that is true. Inductive reasoning seeks to use logic to develop a theory, and deductive reasoning seeks to use logic to prove the theory. The primary way we gain knowledge is through trusted authority. Scientists use all the science before them to build upon. They do not start from scratch. Textbooks, reports, journals, and digests are all means of delivering truth to us.

What is your name? How do you know? How do you know your name? You know it because a trusted authority, your family, told you. You know it because a trusted authority, the State, put it on your birth certificate. You know your name because someone you trust told it to you.

Where is China? Who was the 5th President of the United States? What is the force of gravity? What type of government does the United States have? These questions are answered by a trusted authority or source. You do not deduce China. You have never been to China, so empiricism does not tell you about it. You know where China is by a geography source you trust. Everything we do not personally verify by our senses or deduce ourselves through logic is known by a trusted source.

This is the heart of 'Fake News'. A conservative does not trust liberal news sources and vice/versa. It is also what I do in apologetics. I seek to take people to their source and discern why they trust it.

Most of the time, avenues of truth do not contradict. The Bible does not contradict empirically proven truth. It disagrees with the philosophy of naturalism; however, naturalism is a faith belief and not science. Sometimes our sources of truth disagree. We must choose which one is our final faith. Imagine you are back in Galilee while Jesus walked the earth. You go to the beach. He is walking along the shore and teaching about the Kingdom. You have seen people walk on the shore of a beach. You can scientifically show it is possible. You can deduce it. The Bible teaches it happened. They all agree.

Suddenly, Jesus turns and walks on the water to go get into a boat. Empiricism tells you this does not happen. You never walked on water, nor did any of your friends. You sink. Rational thought can prove it is impossible. The displacement, mass and force of weight on the foot will cause you to sink. The Bible said it happened. So, who are you going to believe?

Believe the Bible. By faith, believe the Bible. I taught Bible at a college. I started the course with evidence for the Scriptures. I presented the evidence and asked, "So, why do we believe the Bible?" The students answered with archaeology, history, anthropology, textual criticism and prophecy examples and reasons. I said, "No. We believe the Bible by faith. These evidences might give you personal credibility, but the final choice is one of faith. By faith, I believe the Bible is the complete revelation of God to humanity. By faith I believe the Bible is inerrant, infallible and inspired. It is by faith. If I build my faith on a shovel (archaeological proof), then a shovel can destroy it as well. I believe the Bible by faith and nothing will ever change that. If the Bible teaches it, then it is truth."

Therefore, I can believe in predestination and volition. If you go to the philosophical end of either of these, then you must concede the other cannot be the truth. I do not use philosophy. The Bible teaches both. I believe both. I believe Jesus is fully human. I believe He is fully God. Math teaches there is no such thing as 200%. If He is 100% human, He is 0% God. If He is 100% God, He is 0% human. The Bible teaches He is 100% God and 100% human. I believe the Bible. The Bible teaches God is sovereign and I have volition. Inductive reasoning leads to fatalism in the first case and a reactive God in the second. The Bible teaches my proactive, sovereign God lets me choose. I believe the Bible.

Believe what the Bible teaches. My personal faith statement

says it like this: The Bible is God's Word to me, and it is my final foundation for faith and life.

Believe the Bible.

LIVE THE WORD.

I counsel a lot of folks because of being a pastor. It is one of my biggest frustrations in ministry. The vast majority of cases, I waste my time counseling. The reason is folks do not want to change. They come to me and share the issue. I listen and give them advice combined with an action plan. I always assign a task. The next week, they come to my office. We chat and I discover they did not do the task. I reassign it. The next week, if they did not do it, I say, "Imagine you go to a doctor because of your heart. He examines you and prescribes medicine with the assurance it will solve the problem. Two weeks later, you return to the doctor because the problem is still there. He examines you and is surprised the medicine did not work. You tell him you did not take it. You filled the prescription, but never took the pill. So, he promises you the medicine will solve the problem and sends you on your way. Three weeks later, you return and the problem is worse. The doctor is shocked. The medicine is proven to heal this issue. He questions you and you admit you did not take the medicine. What do you think the response of the doctor will be? How bad do you want to be healed if you will not follow medical advice? I love and want to help you. You must desire help. Twice I assigned a task for you to do in order to take the journey to healing. You did not do it. I am here. Call me and set up an appointment after you do the task. If you are not willing to put effort into change, we do not need to meet and talk about it."

People often respond in anger to this. I stand my ground. It does no good to anyone for me to tell you how to grow and change if you refuse to do it.

Our family watched Schoolhouse Rock a lot. We know almost all the songs. Remember the motto of Schoolhouse Rock? It says, "Knowledge is power." The world glorifies knowledge. Social media and Internet search engines exist for the purpose of gathering and selling information. Sociologists called my generation the information age. The idea is knowledge, or information, gives us power. This cultural mindset exists in the church as well. Pastors preach sermons full of doctrinal truth. We exposit passages. We teach the meaning of Greek words. We inform people about the cultural setting and historical context of the passage. We hold Bible studies. I googled the word Bible study, and it pulled up 395 million pages. We love to study the Bible. Bible study in a culture glorifying knowledge, confuses many believers. The devil convinced us studying our Bible means we are doing the Bible. We go to church and learn three more Bible truths each Sunday. Yet we have not applied a single truth to our lives this year. I asked a group of pastors at a conference, "Will someone share a Bible truth you learned and applied in the past six months?" No one stood up. No one spoke up. I then asked, "How many of you study and teach the Bible every week?" All the pastors raised their hands.

I taught Bible at a Christian college. At this college, the students divided themselves into two camps. One camp comprised Calvinists. The other camp we're not Calvinists. They believed in human volition. Although everyone professed Christ as Savior, both camps despised the other camp. One day in class, I intentionally stirred up the drama. I took one side as if it were my own, angering the other. I switched viewpoints and took the other side with the same passion. I allowed the students to pick up the debate. At one point, a student stood up and pointed his finger at another student. He yelled, "That is heresy or stupidity! You cannot be a Christian if you believe that!"

I intervened. "Consider this. The Bible states we can know each other by our love. The Bible, Jesus himself, said that we are to bear fruit for God's glory. It does not matter which side of theology you are on at this moment. Almost all of you are in Sin. If your Bible knowledge and doctrine lead you to be a mean jerk, study your Bible a little bit more."

I do not want you to study your Bible. Read that again. I do not want you to study your Bible. I want you to study and apply your Bible. If you do not apply what you learn, you are either a hypocrite, or you are studying the Bible for Knowledge instead of wisdom.

God gave us an incredible gift we too often take for granted.

We have the written, the revealed, the inspired, inerrant Word of the Living God. The Scriptures are not a textbook; they are both a love letter and a guide for life. Through the Bible, we can know all we need to know in order to be the person God desires us to be. I believe the written Word, the Bible, is the greatest gift of God outside of Himself humanity can possess. Your Bible is worth more than your house, car, motorcycle, clothes, equipment...you name it. I did not say your Bible costs more. I said it is worth more. The Bible is our guide to faith and life. The Bible allows me to know God, know myself, and know others. The Bible teaches me about everything in life, from how to forgive, love, and hope to how to manage my money and my time. The Bible reveals God, and my true self to me. It is eternal. God has lifted it higher than His name. The Bible is truly a masterpiece of literature. More than that, it is the inspired Word. It tells us what God has done, what He is doing, and what He is going to do. It tells us how we can be a part of God's work in the world and eternity. It reveals the past and the future and helps us live in the present. God forgave my sins, entered into a relationship with me, and guaranteed me eternity with him in heaven, through revealing his word and my response to it. It is THE WORD.

Do not take this for granted. Don't carry your Bible to church on Sunday, and then not used again till the next Sunday. It should be a part of our everyday life. A part of every moment of our lives.

So, first, read the Bible. This is simply reading. Make it a goal to read it through once a year from now on. Read 10-15 chapters a day. Most of the Bible is a story, so it is easy to read. Read it like you do a novel. Read the story. Look at the characters. Enjoy the literature. Read it. There is no secret here, it is just putting quantity into your mind. Look at your mom's example as I write this. Her goal is to read the Bible in its entirety every month. Now, it is August, and she has only read it six times this year, so she is behind. She told me last week she intends on catching up!

Study the Bible. After reading my introduction, it would seem that I am opposed to Bible study. I am a theologian. I have a Master's degree in theology. I plan to write a book in Spanish on how to study the Bible. I taught high school students and college students how to study the Bible. I believe we should study the Bible. We cannot apply God's truth until we know to God's truth. My point is, to know truth is not the same thing as to apply truth. Study the Bible. Take smaller portions of the Bible and read it with a pencil, paper and purpose. You want to dissect it. Outline the books and the chapters. Look for keywords and cross references. Understand the main point the section is making or the moral of the story. In the text, who is doing what? Ask the adverb questions of the text: Who, What, Where, When, Why, How, and most importantly, What Do I Do With This Information. You do not study to know; you learn to do. I once read we have a low information to action ratio. We get a lot of information, but we do little with it. We have a Low Information to Action Ratio. We become L.I.A.R.S. God doesn't want us to be hearers of the word, even if we are the one speaking. He wants us to be doers. He says when all we do is know the Bible, we deceive ourselves. We are to do it. So, you study the Bible, a topic, book, chapter, section, character, character trait; whatever in order to know what it says so you can do what God wants. The key is to have a notebook, a highlighter, and a pen. Reading is for quantity, Study is for quality. Read the Bible every day and make sure you study it for a few hours every week. The chapter on time management teaches you how to make appointments with God.

Once more, your mom is our role model. She had no type of formal Bible teaching, ever. Yet when we took the over four hundred question Bible exam in order to be SIM missionaries, your mom scored a 96 on that test. A 96! How in the world did she do that without Bible College, on-line classes or seminary? It was a 460-question exam, and your mom only missed about 20 of them. The exam covered the sections of the Scripture, the themes of the Scripture, characters, books, doctrine, prophecy and basic theology. She blew the test out of the water. Why? She studies the Bible. Your mother is a godly, incredibly wise woman because she studies the Bible. Study the Bible.

Memorize the Word. You need to take the Words off of the page and put them into your heart. Memorize not only what God says about specific things, but what God says period. I have memorized 15 books of the New Testament and hundreds of passages and individual verses. I memorize every passage I teach. My personal goal is to memorize the New Testament. Why am I telling you this? Because I want you to see how important it is. This hard work of memorizing Scripture makes the Word readily available for me when I need guidance and/ or help. When the devil tempts you, you cannot argue or rationalize with him. Depend on the Bible, on God's word, for the power to overcome him. You can't say, "I won't do that because of these four reasons." It doesn't work. Say, "The Bible says...." That is what Jesus did in Matthew 4 (which I have memorized). The Bible in your heart is the number one way to avoid sin when tempted. You cannot apply God's word if you do not know God's word.

Meditate on the word. This is the opposite of eastern meditation, which teaches us to empty our minds and try to just go to some neutral zone. It is filling our minds. This connects greatly with memory. In meditating on the word, you think about it, think about it again, go over what it says, what it means, and other verses that connect to it. Think about it as it refers to other passages and how it can apply to your life. Re-word it, paraphrase it, state it in first person terms. Look for insights and truths. I quit listening to music as I drive almost 30 years ago. This isn't because I don't love music. I invest my commute time in praying and meditating on God's word. In a 30-minute drive, I spend 15-20 minutes thinking about a passage of Scripture I am studying and/or memorizing. A lot of my sermon insights and applications of scripture come from this time of meditating as I drive. It is not rare for me to fall asleep at night meditating on a passage of scripture. This gives me good dreams. I also keep a notepad beside my bed to jot down any insights the Holy Spirit gives me.

Hear the word. This is easy, but it is a discipline that you need to do. Let me give you a quick, real life in this moment example. Right now, on my iTunes I have—just counted them—over 470 podcasts from good preachers. I listen to them as I exercise and walk. I make appointments with them in order to better myself. Mom and I have The Bible Experience on our devices. This allows us to listen to the word of God. Sometimes I will put my earphones in and go to sleep listening to the Word. Let others teach you what the Holy Spirit has taught them. In the States, I had a cassette library of over 400 sermons. I listened to every one of them. In seminary, on top of my classes, I listened to two sermons a day on cassette. God uses gifted teachers to speak into our lives.

The main thing is to be a learner and a doer of the Word. You can be WORDly or worldly. Go for the first. Immerse yourself in the Bible so that, if somebody cuts you, you bleed chapter and verse.

KNOW WHO YOU ARE

You know we live two separate lives. We are not hypocritical phonies. We live two lives. It is difficult to explain, and hard to adjust to the reality of it. We are not different people. We have different lives.

Our house in Florida is in a gated community with a swimming pool. In Bolivia we have to purchase water off of a truck and have it delivered to the tank in our yard.

In Florida we have so much water we swim. In Bolivia we only flush the toilet once a day.

In Florida it is green and landscaped. In Bolivia it is brown and wild.

In the States, I am a church member who faithfully attends and supports the staff. In Bolivia I am the pastor of the church.

In Florida, no one knows who I am. In Bolivia I am well known.

In the States, almost everyone I know is wealthier than I am. In Bolivia people think I am super rich because I have a washing machine, a refrigerator and a car.

In the States, I am an average pastor, average speaker, with an average education. In Bolivia I am more highly educated than anyone other than medical doctors., and I am considered an incredible speaker.

In the States, I am the ethnic majority. In Bolivia I am such a minority people stare when we go places.

In the States, no one can imagine what our lives in Bolivia are like, Actually, no one is even that interested to hear about it. In Bolivia, no one can imagine what our lives in the States are like, and to be honest, no one has never even asked us about it.

In the States, I am a conservative Republican. In Bolivia, I cannot talk or write about anything political, nor can I be a member of a political party.

In the States, we can talk for hours and hours about every conceivable subject. I have a PHD level vocabulary. In Bolivia, we have the equivalent of a junior high school vocabulary.

So, who are we then? How do you describe who you are to someone else? I have used David and Joshua as examples on the difficulty of identity. They are Korean men with Jewish names who are American citizens that grew up in Bolivia. So, who are they? Today, David said a friend from work asked him if he identified as a Korean or a White Man. He is Korean but grew up in a White family. The friend wants to know what ethnicity David sees himself to be.

Who are you? As a family, we are currently doing the "Freedom In Christ" video study by Neil Anderson. I love his illustration. If a doctor had to remove my leg, would I still be me? If I lost both legs, would I still be me? If I lost a kidney, am I still me? If I had a heart and lung transplant, am I still me? Is there any point where the doctor removes part of my body and I stop being me? Can I be placed in a specimen jar? No. I am in a body, but my body is not me. Who I am is clothed in this body.

You need to determine right now who you are. The most important aspect is to find your identity in Christ alone. We are not Americans who are Christians. We are Christians who are Americans. I am not a husband who is a Christian. I am a Christian who is married. I am not a father who is a Christian. I am a Christian who has children. Who I am is Christ. Christ needs to be the foremost focus of your life. Allow Him to shape your values and your goals. When you find your identity in Christ, it changes your self-perception and your self-image. You do not have to try to have a high self-image or a low self-image. Find the image of yourself in what Jesus thinks and says about you.

This is so vital. Know who God says you are. You are not who you think you are. You are not who others say you are. You are who God declares you to be. You are accepted, loved, and esteemed. You are the salt of the earth and the light of the world.

You are a member of God's family and a joint heir with Jesus. You are bought with a price and a royal priest. You are the temple of the Holy Spirit. You are God's own child. That is who you are!

Satan and others will lie to you and get you to believe, and act on the belief, that you are someone else. Satan tries to get you to find your identity in other people, peers, activities, and abilities or the opposite of those. Don't let him. Know who you are. You are God's Child.

What group do we use to self-identify? This is so vital, because the person or group we align ourselves with has permission to shape our values. I remember one time we went to Elitch Garden Theme Park in Denver. It was our family together. My belt was a little long and hung about three inches from the buckle. The security guard did not let me in the park. He said the park had a rule against gang insignia. I did not know what he was talking about. As the conversation progressed, I discovered my dangling belt indicated I was a member or supporter of a local street gang. It did not matter I was a father with a family. I had to take my belt off or loop it around in order to enter the park. The guard said the way I dressed indicated I belonged to a group.

As silly as that is, there is truth to it. You will dress like the group you want to identify with. You have heard me say many times the person, people, peer group, whatever we seek to identify with has special power over our lives. Ask yourself, "Who do I want to impress? Who do I want to join? Who do I want to be like?" We give those people permission to shape us, to mold us, to change us. This is why advertising uses athletes and market surveys. Advertisers make us think everyone in the group we want to be part of buys a certain product. This creates a desire in me to buy the same product. The labels on my clothes need to match the labels on the clothes of my peer group.

When we were in Colorado and living in the ghetto, one day I drove home, and self-pity and self-loathing hit me. I looked at our neighborhood as I drove to our rented duplex. There was graffiti everywhere. Windows were boarded shut. Broken-down cars had tires missing. Our duplex was small and ugly. I went into the house and started crying. Denise did not know what was wrong with me. She asked me and I replied, "I am such a horrible husband and father. I cannot even provide for my family. We live below the federal poverty line. Our neighborhood is ugly and dangerous. We have nothing of value. I am such a failure." Instead of arguing with me, she went to the bookshelf and got my Bible off of it. She handed it to me and asked, "Is this what God says about you? Does He think you are a failure? Can you show me in the Bible where you concluded the socio-economic level of your neighborhood determines who you are?"

I was instantly hit with conviction. I was not judging myself by the Word. I was not looking at my identity through the cross. I was looking at what I thought others thought about me because of my living conditions. I had to rethink. My self-worth is not determined by my net worth. Who I am is determined by who my Creator has said I am, and how He has created me.

As much as you can, avoid putting labels on yourself and on other people. I once read on social media a quote I loved. It said, "Labels tell me who I may hate." Do not look at people as Republicans or Democrats. Try not to see rich or poor. Don't put people into theological camps such as Calvinist or Arminian. You need to see yourself as a child of God. Look at other people and see them as someone who knows Christ, or someone who needs to know Him. The other things do not matter. It is not eternally important for you or them. I believe growing up biculturally has helped you see labels are temporary and cultural. We need to focus on the eternal, both for the label we put on ourselves and the ones we put on others.

Therefore, see yourself as a child of God. Once more, you are redeemed and beloved. You are the salt and light of the world. You are forgiven and justified. You are a member of God's own family and part of a Royal Priesthood. You are part of the eternal church of Christ. God personally lives in you and you in Him. You are chosen by Him. You have been adopted by God Himself. You are a citizen of heaven and complete in Him. The Bible teaches when we become Christians, we are new creations. We are absolutely unique in the universe. There is something about us that makes us phenomenal. We now have access to more power than Satan himself and are above the angels. This is why the devil wants us to forget who we are in Christ. View yourself as God sees you. He has declared you righteous, holy, and of eternal value.

Remember what we learned about the price God paid for you. He gave the only thing that cost Him anything, and it cost Him everything. God, not you, God decided you were of such value He would give Himself for you. You are of infinite and eternal value because God declared you to be when Christ died for you. Never let yourself, Satan, or the world convince you that you are worthless. God, through the act of sending His Son and buying you, determined you to be priceless. Learn to see yourself through the eyes of the Father. Learn to think of yourself as who you really are. Don't conform to the group, be shaped by the reality of what is inside. You are the image of God. Inside of you is the Holy Spirit, Who is moment by moment helping you live on the outside what is inside. Be who you are. Real hypocrisy is when a child of God pretends to be something or someone else. So, you need to stop acting. Let the fact you are a royal member of the household and kingdom of God determine what you think, how you act, what you do.

For example, many times when we meet someone we want them to like us, so we are thinking about how we look, sound, or how we think they perceive us. When you know, without a doubt, that you are accepted in Christ and part of His family, then you can, when you meet someone, be thinking about them. You can be praying about how you can bless, serve, encourage, or help them. When you are face to face with a temptation to sin, stop and think about who you really are in Christ. The temptation is targeting someone who lives only in the flesh. You are not merely in the flesh. You are a spiritual being with flesh. You are a child of God. You are a saint. The real you... the genuine you...the authentic you...doesn't want to wade in the muck and mire, you are a clean and holy person. Let who you are determine what you do!

This doesn't mean you don't connect or be a part of groups here as well. You have to be a part of a group. God created us to live in a community. This is one purpose of the local church. It is to give you a community of fellowship. However, your primary source of identity should never come from your peer group, even if it is the local church. Your primary source of identity is Jesus Christ. He died for you. He lives in you. Let His death and resurrection be who you are.

When Seth died, I posted this on social media. "My identity and purpose are in the truth I am a Son of God, not the father of Seth. If my identity was found in being a parent, then my identity died with him. If my identity and purpose were found in my earthly relationships, I am now afloat with no purpose. My identity and purpose are found in the truth I am a child of God. I am a son of God who has lost my child." Your identity in Christ keeps you focused when the world shakes.

There is more to who you are than just your source of identity. We build upon that foundation. The next thing to do is to look at who God has individually created you to be and seek to be and become that person. There is a saying, "You can do anything you want!" It is not true. It is also not what we should pursue. We can do anything God wants us to do. His will is our goal. We find His will as we discover who He created us to be. God has worked through all eternity to bring you to this place in this time. He has made YOU. YOU are unique. Discover who He made you to be.

One way to do this is to identify your personality type. There are a lot of different tests and methods of doing this. Know what your personality is and what strengths and weaknesses that type of personality has.

Look at your spiritual gifts and use them in the church. God gifted you uniquely in order to bring Him glory by using those gifts. As you use them, you understand who you are in Christ and in fellowship.

I also believe God is sovereign and works His will through our experiences. God allowed you to grow up bi-cultural and bi-lingual. He had you live on the mission field among the poor for a reason. Find out how that and other experiences have shaped you.

God gave you natural abilities and learned abilities. These come together to determine who you are. Finally, what excites you? What do you really love to do? What moves your heart? That is part of who you are. I recommend you spend time each year in self-reflection. Consider how God is working through your personality, spiritual gifts, experiences, passion and abilities. He is molding you into the image of His Son and into a man/woman that can bring Him unique glory.

Another important thing to do is to identify your values. Make a list of what is truly important to you. I will point out in the chapter on time management we should live these values out in our lives. Your value statement is not your doctrinal statement. It is simply a way of saying what you believe you should prioritize in life. I will list the value statement of our family here for an example. You can look at how we raised you and see that these values were the priority of our lives.

Core Values Of Holman Ministry

- To know and follow Jesus Christ is the single most important thing in all of eternity. In everything we do, the gospel will be proclaimed clearly and in a culturally relevant manner.
- The Bible is the revealed Word of God and is our sole and final authority.
- God's basic unit is the family. Strong families produce strong churches that change nations. We will seek to be and to help other families become, strong and stable homes.
- The church is the body of Christ and the Holy Spirit has uniquely gifted her to accomplish His purpose. All we do is done in, with, through and for local

churches.

- The Kingdom of God is the purpose of our ministry, therefore we will partner with local churches and other evangelical ministries if our partnership can enable either them or us to further God's Kingdom.
- Everything is dependent upon Spirit-filled, Christ-like leadership. We will seek to disciple and equip the leaders of the church(es).
- The heart of discipleship is becoming like Jesus Christ and bearing the fruit of the Holy Spirit. Our discipleship is focused on character and life-change.
- God's truth is eternal and changeless. We are not. We will seek to constantly grow and become better both as individual followers of Christ and as a ministry. All we do is open to change if change will produce more fruit.
- God wants us to invest all we are into His Kingdom. Therefore, anything we can do and the Holy Spirit leads us to do is our ministry. Our question, when presented with an opportunity is: "Can we help with this?" If our spiritual gifts, resources and abilities can be used to further God's Kingdom, we seek to invest them.
- We seek to be General Practitioners rather than Specialist. By this we mean we want to constantly be open to what God is doing and how we can join Him instead of focusing solely on one aspect of ministry.
- God desires for the local church to be the driving force in reaching the community and missions to the world. We seek to be actively involved in both serving and equipping the local church.
- Ministry cost money. We want to develop means to produce income that can be invested into the gospel of Jesus Christ.
- Followers of Jesus should meet the needs of the poor. We will seek to provide for their needs both because

37

of the gospel of Jesus Christ (He has told us to) and in order to proclaim the gospel of Jesus Christ.

- The heart of leadership is to enable and to delegate. It is more important to help things get accomplished than it is to do them yourself. Our ministry will seek to multiply our effectiveness through enabling others to impact the Kingdom of God. The more a leader grows, the more a leader accomplishes through others.

Look back at your life in our home, both as a pastor's kid and as a missionary kid. You can see all we accomplished was focused not on our theology, but on this practical application of our theology. I will talk more about this in the section on prioritizing your values. The point is to know what is important to you, and then to do what is important to you. If you do not determine your values, then you will live out the values of others. God created you and gave you this heart in order for you to live it out. Never try to be someone you are not in order to have friends. You want your friends to love you for who you are, not who you pretend to be.

STAY CONNECTED
TO YOUR FAMILY

We love Legos. Thirty-one years of parenting eleven children gave us a lot of opportunities to purchase them. I estimate we have over $2,000 worth of Legos. They are expensive. The heart of good Lego play is connecting. You connect the Legos to each other. You connect them in the right order. Once connected, they make a solid object. Disconnected and you step on them barefoot going to the bathroom at night. A Lego by itself is trash. Legos connected correctly are art.

There are currently four of you left at home. Hope and Joy will leave us to start their own lives this year. So, seven kids left the nest. I have a question for you. Don't you love the fact your older siblings call you every week? Isn't it fun to play D&D with your siblings on two continents and two different states? It is awesome! Your older siblings all visited us in Bolivia after they lived in the States. They call us all the time. When we are in Florida, they almost never go home. We literally looked at the calendar this week. We have had company, mainly older siblings, in our home for ten weeks without a break. Over seventy days of company. It honestly gets a little overwhelming, but I would not trade it for the world. Your siblings understand they, like a Lego, need to be connected to the family. We need each other.

You are leaving our authority and establishing your own home. We believe once someone reaches the age of 20, in the eyes of God, they are a household. You are leaving our household to establish your own. You are your own person and your own family. Mom and I have no authority over you. You have seen us relate to your older siblings as they left. We do not even give advice unless they ask it.

However, we, your family, are still extremely important in your personal growth and spiritual journey. God put you into our family for a purpose. He could have placed you in any family in any time period of the existence of man. Yet, He put you in my family as my child. There is a definite reason for this. Your family (us) will always play a role in your life. We will always be your parents. I am not talking about honoring us, that you should and will do. I mean, let your family be a part of your present, not just a part of your past. Ask us for advice, and we will seek to give you sound, wise and biblical advice. Ask us for help and we will try to help you. Invite us into your life, and we will accept the invitation. Have your brothers and sisters be part of your life. Invite them to stay with you. Talk to them on the phone. Write them emails. Send them gifts. You are a great influence in their lives, help them live for Jesus.

I am going to mention friends in a moment but let me address this a little now. Your mother and I want to be your best friends. Your life will be shaped by the people you think are important, the ones you listen to, and the ones you want to be like. They will determine what you value and what you do. There is no one on earth who wants more for you than we do. We have no selfish desire to be your friend because of what we can get out of it. We simply want to help you, to influence you towards Jesus, and to encourage you to become who God created you to become. No lectures, just an honest love and desire for you to be a success. Let us be there for you.

Look at your mother's relationship to Paul and Darlene as an example. After we were married, and now for 36 years, we are our own family. Paul and Darlene never told us what to do, and do not try to butt into our business. Yet almost every day for 29 years, Denise talks to them. We have vacationed together many times. We have asked them for professional, financial and spiritual advice. They are our best friends. As I write this, your mom is in Texas taking care of grandma because she has CoVid. We are middle-aged adults with our own grandchildren, yet we remain connected to our parents. Stay connected. It is a blessing.

FORGIVE OTHERS

Mom and I owned a dog shortly after we got married. Our yard did not have a fence, so we had to keep the dog chained to a rotating stake in the yard. There was plenty of room. He had a twenty-foot circle to use. He did something all the time. Something would excite him, and he would take off running at full speed. He hit the end of the chain and flipped backwards to the ground. He never learned the chain only let him run twenty feet. Every single time he expected a different outcome. He was a real-life example of the character, Barnyard Dawg, from Looney Tunes. This is a good illustration of not forgiving others. When we do not forgive, we drive a stake in the ground at the point of the offense. We can never go very far from it. It holds us and chains us to the wrong committed against us. Unlike the cartoon, it is not funny.

Remember building the church in the Amazon Basin, at Ushve? People do not realize the sheer billions of insects which live in the jungle. We used insect repellant. We had mosquito netting. We wore long sleeve shirts and tucked our pants into our socks. At end of the week, Joshua won the mosquito bite contest. He had over 100 bites from his neck to one wrist. Mom was second place with seventy mosquito bites on one arm. Mercy was five and the rest of you were young as well. Mom said, thousands of times in the next month, "Don't scratch!" The bites were miserable, and it is difficult to overcome the urge to scratch the itch. Mom warned you about what would happen if you kept scratching the scabs off. The bites do not heal correctly. You turn a bite into a wound and keep reopening it. The end result is infection, and you would have scars. A couple of you did not listen and you have a few scars. You will live the rest of your life, not with the bites, but with your response to the bites. The mosquito did not scar you. You did it to yourself. Bitterness and refusing to forgive others are like this story. Someone hurt you. You do not forgive. You reopen the wound again and again. You think about it and retell the story to yourself. You do not let it heal. The issue in your life changes from the hurt you experienced into the damage you do to yourself in response to the hurt. It is no longer the offense of the other person. It is what you did with the offense.

The Bible makes it clear we live in a fallen world full of fallen people. You are going to be hurt. People are going to hurt you on purpose and on accident. Some will hurt you because they are mean, others because they are ignorant, and others because they are hurt themselves. Hurt people hurt people. People will hurt you. People will say things to you and about you and will do things to you. Friends will betray you and family will let you down.

The Bible also makes it clear when you are hurt, you have one option available for you. You must forgive them. Instantly, totally, and unconditionally. Forgiveness is the only course of action for a follower of Christ. You forgive them because God forgave you. They don't deserve it; they don't earn it, and they don't merit it. You don't forgive because you are a forgiving person. You forgive them because God loves them. You forgive them because you can see past the thing they did to their own need for Calvary. You forgive them because your Lord told you to.

You have heard us say this a gazillion times. We are forgiven sinners, forgiving sinners. Remember, sinners respond sinfully to sin. You are not a sinner! You are a saint. You do not respond sinfully to sin. You respond in a Christlike manner to sin. That means you forgive it.

In your life, how many times did you hear mom or me ask you for forgiveness? How many times did you hear us say we forgive you? Forgiveness is a way to free yourself from hurts of the past. Let me tell you how important it is. When Seth was dying in the hospital room, I leaned over and whispered into his ear. I said several things, but this was one of them. "Son, I want you to know I forgive you. If there is anything in your life where you feel like you have hurt me, I forgive you. If you think you wronged me, I forgive you. If in any way whatsoever you think I am offended or let down by you, I forgive you. Also, if I have hurt or wronged you in any way, please forgive me. If I did do something I should not have, or did not do something I should have, please forgive me. Step into eternity forgiven and forgiving."

Forgiveness is the foundation of our faith. It is part of the reason Jesus went to the cross. It is the symbol. It is the call. We are to forgive.

Bitterness is an acid that eats through the container carrying it. I read a quote once that said, "Bitterness is drinking poison and hoping your enemy dies." When we do not forgive, it messes up all of our relationships, starting with Jesus. You forgive. Be a forgiver. It frees you from living in the hurt and in the past. It helps you become like Jesus, and it allows you to focus on what God is doing in your life and in theirs. It lets you look to the heavens instead of to your hurt. Forgiveness is not only a gift to the person you are forgiving, but also a blessing to you.

So, how do you do it? Simple. Focus on the truth the Holy God of all creation forgave you. The Perfect and Sinless God forgives you constantly and eternally. So, you remember your forgiveness. The next thing you do is forgive them immediately and completely. Make the choice to forgive the moment they offend you. Do not wait to be asked. Do not wait to feel like it. By faith, you act now. Immediate forgiveness allows you to proactively respond to them. After that, every time you remember it, or the enemy reminds you of it, forgive them again. Forgiveness is a one-time event repeated a lot.

Forgive. Forgive again. Then keep doing it till heaven.

RESOLVE CONFLICT

At Christmas time in 2017, we were in the States. It was our year for celebrating Christmas. Everybody came to our house. All of the children with their spouses, as well as Grandma and Grandpa stayed with us. It was about 11 pm and all of you kids sat in the living room. You laughed, talked and told stories to each other about growing up in our home. Mom and I listened with joy from the other room. I went to you guys and said, "I want you to be honest with me. I am serious. I want the truth. How many times in your life did you see or hear me and your mom fight? How many times did you witness an argument?"

You know the answer. You were there. Not one of you ever heard, saw or knew of a conflict between me and mom. I expected to hear you say zero, or maybe once. We celebrated 36 years of marriage this year. In those 36 years, we can only remember two times when we had a sinful conflict. I define sinful conflict as both of us treating the other person sinfully. Sinfully responding to a sinful action. This may surprise you to hear the following sentence. Mom and I have conflict a lot. We have conflict several times a week.

Conflict is normal. It is part of life. It is natural. Conflict occurs in a relationship every time there are two desired outcomes. I want to eat Mexican food. Your mother wants to eat Chinese food. We do not agree on where to eat. That is a conflict. A friend asked you to come over. Mom wants to let you. I think you need to stay home and do schoolwork. That is a conflict. When my will or desire is different than your mother's will or desire, we have a conflict.

Understand this. Conflict is never a problem. Responding sinfully and selfishly to conflict is the problem. It is not the conflict. It is how I respond and seek to resolve the conflict which hurts relationships. Your mother and I seek to resolve our conflicts correctly.

The first thing is the main thing in everything. Remember your purpose. Our purpose is to glorify God. In everything we do, He is to be lifted up and honored. My purpose in the midst of this conflict ought to be to glorify God in how I resolve it. My thoughts, words, and actions are to bring Him glory. My purpose is to glorify God, not get my way.

I cover this in the chapter on spiritual fruit. Conflict bumps me and allows me to see what spills from my heart. It shakes my tree and lets my fruit hit the ground. God uses other people, my relationships, and the circumstances of life to help me see how much I need Jesus. Conflict reveals my heart and motivations. The purpose of this conflict is to help me glorify God and become like Jesus. If I focus on these two things, most conflicts are resolved before they begin.

Remember, the relationship is more important than the conflict. I like to say, "We are better than Me." My goal is to build the relationship. It might be with mom, you guys, or a coworker. I want to help them in their walk with Christ more than prove my point.

When a conflict occurs, before it is escalated to verbally resolving it, ask yourself, "Does this conflict need to be expressed? Will it help our relationship to determine a winner?" Your mom and I, more often than not, avoid unnecessary conflict. Mom says something to me, and I believe she is mistaken. Perhaps she tells a story about Hope in Bolivia. I know the story and I think it was Joy instead of Hope. How necessary is it for me to interrupt the story in order to correct this detail? It is not. I avoid the conflict because the conflict is irrelevant. Yet how many times do people argue and hurt each other over something like this? Go back to the example I used about wanting to eat at two different places. Do I need to fight for Mexican food? Or do I know, in the future, I will eat Mexican food? Is eating a burrito instead of an egg roll important enough to me to hurt your mom or our relationship? I'll let your mom choose the food. The conflict is resolved.

Humility is another great way to defuse and resolve conflict. Whenever I have a conflict with your mom over an event that happened, when she thinks one thing and I think another, one of us is right. The other one is wrong. Here is the kicker. We both think we are the one who is right. We both believe the other person is wrong. I do not argue if I think I am wrong. So, she thinks she is right. I think I am right. One of us is wrong about being right. Humility tells me there is just as much of a chance I am wrong, yet I think I'm right, as there is, she is wrong yet thinks she is right. Humility acknowledges I might be the one who is wrong. I decide to just let the discussion end. You hear one of us say something along these lines, "I am not sure you are right, but I know I am usually wrong. It doesn't matter." The Bible says love covers a myriad of sins and it is to a man's glory to overlook a fault. If I am secure in Christ and love you, I do not need to prove to you I am right. If I put the relationship above myself, I do not need to argue an irrelevant point or die on a hill not worth fighting for.

If the conflict happens before you can defuse it, or if you feel it is important enough to pursue, remember to watch your heart. Do not allow sinful thoughts, words or actions to be on your side of the conflict highway. Examine your heart and motivations. I like to ask myself, "Why is it important for me to get my desired outcome in this conflict?" A lot of times it is. Parenting is a great example. You and I had many conflicts over the years. Those conflicts were the result of you being a child. I sought to train and help you love Jesus. I disciplined you for sin and disobedience. I needed to resolve the conflict with my desired outcome because you needed to grow. In the workplace, it can be important to resolve the conflict in order to accomplish the job. I just like to examine my heart and make sure I am not seeking my way because I am selfish.

Stay on topic. Focus on the activity or event and not the other person. Discuss what happened and what needs to happen. Do not assume you know what they thought or the motivation of their heart. Discuss your goals and listen to theirs with an open mind. Remember, the ultimate goal is to resolve the conflict to the satisfaction of both people and the glory of God. It is not to win.

More often than not, conflict is avoided by one person choosing to not escalate it. In marriage conferences, people have told me, "You want us to be a doormat. I will not let them walk all over me." My response is this. "I am not a doormat. I am a set of stairs. I am not letting you walk on me. I am helping you attain new heights. I want to serve you and bless you. I want to lift you up, not put you down. If my choosing to not fight in this moment blesses our relationship, I will choose it every time."

ABIDE IN THE HOLY SPIRIT.

We just got out of the pool. We had an underwater swimming contest. I did not win. I don't know why, because I am a big guy, but I cannot hold my breath very long. I can only be under about 45 seconds before I have to come up and get another breath. However, one time I went over 150' deep for over 30 minutes. We were in a submarine. The UK announced a new stealth submarine. It has a newly engineered nuclear engine and can stay underwater for 25 years. It only needs to surface every three months to restock on food for the sailors. How did mom and I stay underwater for 30 minutes? How can a sailor live underwater for three months? We were not holding our breath. The sailors live, abide in the submarine. It protects and provides for them. It prevents harm from the environment. The submarine meets their needs.

Most Christians live the Christian life the same way we swim underwater. We take a deep breath of Jesus and hold that breath as long as we can hold it. We step away and take another breath. We take a breath of Jesus in our quiet time. It runs out. We take another breath, listening to Christian music on our commute. It runs out. The next day we repeat the cycle. Then we take another breath. We should live our Christian life like sailors on a submarine. We don't take a breath of Jesus. We live in the Spirit. We abide in Him.

At this very moment, who or what has the most influence on your next decision? Be honest. On a moment-by-moment basis, how much actual influence does the Eternal and Unbroken Presence of Jesus Christ have on your life? Does your social media presence agree with your answer?

I am not asking if you are in sin. This is not talking about making a moral choice or not. My question is, how much influence does the Presence of Jesus have in your life, on your life, this moment. I believe the answer is very little.

Our morality, politics, capitalism, religion, our tradition, family may have tremendous influence on us. The particular news channel or talk show we follow influences us. Our peer group and church influence us. All these things help shape us. They have formulated my worldview. My question is more proactive.

How often during the day do you think of, listen to, or talk to Jesus?

We have had several of our friends mimic what we do on our sixteenth birthday in creating the book for their kids. They asked me to write letters to their children who are turning the corner and heading towards adulthood. This is what I tell them.

The most important thing that you can do, in my opinion, hands down with no exception is this: Abide in Christ. The Bible expresses this in many different ways. Be filled with the Holy Spirit. Be led by the Holy Spirit. Abide in Me. Abide in love. Walk in love. Walk in the light. Abide in My love. Walk in the Spirit. Abide in the Vine. Etc. These mean the same thing. In a nutshell, let me summarize it.

At every moment, with every breath, and during every thought, seek to consciously acknowledge your dependence upon Jesus.

God created us to find everything we need, want or desire in Jesus. The great error of Christianity is trying to find purpose in any other thing. The essence of sin is trying to find purpose, pleasure, or satisfaction in something other than God. I believe many good people get caught up in consciously avoiding some particular behavior, or consciously imitating some other behavior. The end result of this is measuring ourselves by what we do or don't do. But, consciously acknowledging your dependence upon God means right now, in this moment, you are humbly recognizing that you need His strength, His grace, His power, His presence. You need Him. It means you know He is God, and you must have His reality in your life.

It isn't looking at your life by what you have done, are doing, or want to do. It is looking at who God is and what He is doing in your life. When someone hurts or wrongs you, consciously acknowledge you are dependent upon Christ in order to forgive them and respond appropriately. When you are tempted to sin, consciously acknowledge you are dependent upon Christ and you need His power and protection to deliver you from the sin temptation is drawing you towards. When you have multiple opportunities in front of you, consciously acknowledge your dependence upon Christ and you need His wisdom to guide you. This phrase, 'Consciously acknowledging your dependence upon Christ', contains within its practice: humility, faith, grace, prayer, worship, confession, etc. It holds the theological truths of humanity, salvation, and sanctification. It is the root of true spiritual discipline, and the method of spiritual growth. Jesus said it this way, I am the vine, you are the branches; he who abides in Me and I in him, he bears much fruit, for apart from Me you can do nothing (John 15.5). This is the most important principle of Scripture I have ever learned or taught. This is what you must learn to do, and you learn to do it by doing it. Every decision, good, bad, or indifferent—make with prayer. Every opportunity, relationship, and choice...make with a conscious, if possible verbal, prayer for God's guidance, strength, purpose and glory. This is Spirit Filled Living, and it is the only true Life. Choose to acknowledge your absolute dependence upon Him in this breath. Seek His Presence and Wisdom. Pray without ceasing. Walk, that means every step, in dependence upon the Holy Spirit.

ATTEMPT GREAT THINGS FOR GOD.

I love to remind you guys of the Ushve church. One day I was at my desk and Hope came to me. She was 11 years old. She said, "We were praying, and I thought of all the poor people. So many poor people do not have a church. They meet under a tree or in the sun. I told the girls. We decided God told us to build a church for poor people."

I said, "That is nice, honey." I thought no more about it. I basically blew you gals off as silly.

That night your mom said, "What if God told the girls to build a church? If it is God working, the person He uses doesn't have to have credentials. God works in His children. He might have spoken to the girls, and you ignored them."

I saw her wisdom. The next day I asked you about it. I pointed out that it would cost over $10,000. I said none of you had any means of raising money. Your responses were so full of faith. "God owns the cattle on a thousand hills. This is easy for Him." "God can do anything. He can provide the money." "If God said do it, it will be done."

I was actually taken aback by your total confidence in His call.

Fast forward less than one year. I did not help you. On your own, you raised over $12,000 and we were in the Amazon Jungle area. We flew in a mission aviation plane and spent a week building their church.

You walked by faith. You expected God to work.

Look back at the title of this chapter. I need to warn you. This is the title of the sermon I preached the day God called us to the mission field. It was not a sermon on missions, even though the quote is from William Carey. I did a series called "Great Expectations". It was on faith. I asked this question in the last message of the series. "What do you expect God to do in your life? What would God do if you went to Him and said, 'Lord, there are no, No's in my life? I will do anything you ask me expect me to do." At that moment, during my message, the Holy Spirit said, "Go to the mission field." Over and over, He said it. It distracted me from preaching. On the way home from church, mom asked me what I wanted to do. She meant for the rest of the afternoon. I remember it distinctly. We were on Mountain Road, going around the sloping curve with the huge meadow to our left. I said, "Go to the mission field."

She did not miss a beat. She asked me, "Are you serious?"

"Yes. I think I am."

She pulled out her bulletin from the previous week. In the margin she wrote, "I need to be ready to follow Christ, no matter what He says. Even if it means selling all I have and going to the mission field."

We fasted and prayed. That was in 2006.

What do you expect God to do? The challenge I issued to my church, and now that I am issuing to you, is this. What are you attempting to do for God? What do you expect God to do in your life? If today, God met all of your expectations, what would be different from yesterday? Most Christians have no expectations of God. We honestly don't expect Him to do anything in our lives except let us go to heaven. The corollary is most of us not only have no faith in God working in our lives; we apply no faith to our lives. We do not try to do anything for God.

This title says it all. Attempt great things for God. Don't measure your life by what you can do, and don't limit yourself to trying those things that you can reasonably expect success from. Don't live a $5 life because you have $6 in your pocket. Look at your life from God's perspective. He put you here, and He did not put you here for little things or little thinking. He wants to use you. Like those fishermen who followed Jesus, God wants to expand your world. You will no longer catch fish, you will catch men! You will no longer fish in the waters of lake Galilee. You are responsible for the world!

God wants to open your eyes, expand your horizons, rock your world and use you to change the world of others. In order to accomplish this, you must attempt great things. They will not just happen. You will not win the world from your social media. You must venture forth into it. Look up and then look around. God can use you to do more than you can ever imagine.

I am a redneck from a poor family of rednecks. I was a trouble-making druggie. My only goal in life was to be rich, and I had no moral compass to direct how I arrived at wealth. A poor man from a small town has been to almost 20 countries on five continents. I have preached and been translated into 10 different languages. God has brought several thousand people to faith in Him through using me. I have nothing to offer. I offered it to God, and He made it something incredible.

Never limit your life or your efforts by basing them on your resources. God wants you to do God-sized things that require God-sized resources.

I am amazed at how so many of our discipleship programs ignore walking or living by Faith. In the Bible the word 'faith' and its derivatives are used 430 times. The word 'believe' and its derivatives are used 257 times. The word 'trust' and its derivatives are used 181 times. Add those up and you see God refers to us having faith, believing and trusting over 800 times. It is a big deal to God. God says we should live by faith, we should walk by faith and without faith we cannot please Him! Now, ask yourself this question: What does it mean to live by faith and am I doing it?

I have asked this question to over fifty mature Christian men. Not once did they reply with total confidence in either their knowledge of what it meant to walk by faith, or actually doing it. The vast majority of believers do not have a developed theology of faith. Despite the truth God says we cannot please

Him without it, most discipleship curriculums either ignore it or just lightly touch upon it. Usually, we leave faith at the cross. We are saved by faith, but we do not live by faith. We believe and trust the Person and Work of Christ for the forgiveness of sins. After that moment, how often does our faith direct our steps?

I use Hebrews 11 to develop this definition of faith.

Faith is a total trust in the existence and character of God as revealed in the Bible.

Faith is a total trust: Notice how firm faith is in verse one. It is an assurance and a conviction. The word assurance refers to a foundation or solid rock. It signifies no doubt. The word conviction is a legal term of evidence. It is proof demonstrated. Our faith is not as it has been said, "A blind man in a dark room looking for a black cat that isn't there". Faith is real. Faith is more real than sight. Faith is a total trust with no wavering.

Faith is a total trust in the existence...of God: This is the part of the definition that really lept out of the Scripture and into my heart when I was studying this. I taught a series on faith at my church, and I spent an entire message, 45 minutes, on this one truth. God exists. He who comes to God must believe that He is. This seems strange. Of course you believe in God, but do you believe He is? How much influence on your life did the Existence of God have yesterday? Does the Existence and Presence of God manage your thoughts, attitudes, words or actions?

God says we must believe that HE IS. Faith is me consciously acknowledging the Existence and Presence of God. How do I walk by faith? I allow the truth that God Exists, and He is here to influence my every thought, word and deed.

Faith is a total trust in the existence and character of God as revealed in the Bible: The Bible does not just tell us that God Exists. It tells us Who God Is and What He Is Like. We can know God personally and we can learn about His Character. I believe that the Loving, Merciful, Just, Holy, Good, Kind, Giving, Forgiving, All Knowing, All Powerful, Ever Present God is with me, right now, at this moment. My actions should not be based upon my character, but upon His. That is faith.

Faith is a total trust in the existence and character of God as revealed in the Bible.

I have already answered this, but what does it mean to live by or to walk by faith? It means in this moment, in this breath, right now with this heart attitude, I acknowledge that the God of the Bible Exists and He is Here. I orient my life around His Existence, Character and Presence. I allow my decisions, all of them, to be determined by His Existence and His Presence. As I understand Him, then I live more and more for Him. That is called following, or discipleship.

In the chapter on 'Abiding', I asked this question: On a moment-by-moment basis, how much actual influence does the Eternal and Unbroken Presence of Jesus Christ have on your life?

This same question allows us to walk by faith. I will re-word it.

On a moment-by-moment basis, how much actual influence does the Existence, Character and Presence of God have on your life?

LIVE BY GRACE

In 2015, we built the house for Adrian's parents. If you remember, his mother was one of the high witches in the Cochabamba coven. They hated Christians. God used your mom's love to break through to her. Both parents gave their lives to Christ. There is an interesting story. Adrian was thirteen years old. He attended a church camp at Camp Kewiña. His mother attended a statewide coven meeting for the witches in our province. Adrian gave his life to Jesus. A few hundred miles away, the head witch stopped the meeting. She looked at Adrian's mom and said, "Your son did something horrible. Go home now." The witch knew God saved Adrian. Adrian's mom and dad beat him and tried to get him to recant. He would not. They cast a spell on him. God protected him.

That phrase, "cast a spell" is what the Apostle Paul used in Galatians. He spoke to believers who lived in the same manner most of us live today. They came to Christ by faith. but After salvation, they lived as if under the law. The apostle Paul said it could only be one of two things. They were under a witch's spell, or they were stupid. Legalistic living is replacing a life of faith with a life of indebted servitude. I have to work. I must earn this salvation I received. God said legalism is stupid or demonic.

As you seek to serve the Lord, one of the greatest traps we can fall into is to evaluate our lives by what we are doing, should do, could do, etc. We end up, if we are not careful, in establishing a set of rules in our religiosity we must follow. Now I am not talking about Spirit-led convictions you choose to apply because the Lord has told you to. Nor am I talking about practicing the Spiritual Disciplines. Do not allow your convictions or the disciplines to become your standard of spirituality (see the section of fruit). Discipline yourself for a purpose (Timothy says discipline yourself for the purpose of godliness).

When I say live by grace, I mean let God's grace saturate your life. Live, not in the shadow of, but in the light of Calvary. God's grace is there for you. I define Grace as the "God freely meeting my needs through Himself and His power."

All the components of this definition are at work in Biblical grace.

It is God initiated. God is the one that dispenses grace. It begins within Him. True grace comes from God to me. There are a lot of theological terms to describe this truth. God's grace comes from God to me and not the other way around.

God Freely Meeting My Needs. I do not earn the favor of God, nor do I pay it off after He gives it to me. I cannot stand the song lyrics that say we are such a debtor to grace. We are not. It was a gift, not a loan. I cannot do anything that will make God give me grace. It is the very fact I need grace that makes it available. If I did not need grace, then I would simply earn a wage.

God Freely Meeting My Needs Through Himself. Please stop and think about this. I believe this aspect is the most over-looked part of grace. We look at grace as simply an activity of God or a gift God gives us. It is more than that. Our focus is not on the gifts it is on the giver. Grace is not merely God initiated. It is an actual attribute of God. Grace is not just God giving me something; it is God giving me Himself. When I need the grace of God, I find it in the Person of God.

Don't live in your own strength. Don't live a life of behavior modification or performance-based acceptance. Live life in, for and through grace. It is so easy to define the Christian life by a set of rules, of do's and don'ts, of have to's and can'ts. It is so easy to let your prayer life, your devotions, your Bible studies, and your church attendance become the sum total of your life. Living by grace means you always remember these things have a purpose. They are not the purpose. They will not meet your needs, nor will they fulfill your life. Only God and His power can. Living by grace ties back into Holy Spirit filled living, because it is God freely meeting my needs through HIMSELF and His power. Grace isn't God giving me the power I need to do something. It is God helping me do it. It is God doing it for me and through me. I don't need God's power. I need God. God's power can move things, God changes me. Grace always remembers you are not strong enough to attain, nor do you merit, the blessings of God. It is always saying, "God, because of the life and death and life of Jesus, You promised to never leave me. I need You to help me, change me, work through me, etc. because I cannot do it without You." Grace always results in us experiencing the reality of Jesus Christ and God receiving the glory.

Practice prayer, study, memorization, worship, etc., but always remember that they are a means to an end. It is like taking a bus. You don't just take a bus because other people are on the bus. You take a bus because you are going somewhere. Your destination also determines which bus you take. The disciplines are designed to take you into the presence of God. They do not take the place of God. Grace keeps the disciplines in perspective.

BE A PERSON
OF PRAYER

In 1986, I surrendered to the ministry. I set up an appointment with my pastor. At the meeting, I asked this man whom I respected so much how to be successful in ministry. I said, "I want to open my life up to you. Tell me what I need to do in order to succeed in ministry and I will do it. I trust you."

He replied. "Joe, there are three things you must do. First, pray. Second, pray. Third, pray."

I left the meeting slightly disappointed. I expected a deep insight or some wonderful secret. Move to the present time, thirty-five years later. He was correct. It is prayer.

Prayer works. Prayer changes me, you, others, and circumstances. A famous theologian once said, "Prayer is the slender nerve that moves the muscle of omnipotence." I was once told, "It may be a coincidence, but it sure seems like there are a lot more coincidences when I pray."

Prayer works. Prayer is vital. Prayer connects you to God, conforms you to His will, and helps you participate in His plan. Prayer brings the presence and power of God into the circumstances of your own life and the lives of others.

Pray. Pray more. Spend time each day praying. I used to, and I am doing this again, spend 1 hour a day in prayer, one day a month, 8 hours in unbroken prayer. I never made it over five hrs without giving up. Prayer is hard work. Pray without ceasing by always looking for things, people, circumstances and situations to ask help, give thanks or praise God for. Also, pray every day in your own private devotions. I think it is interesting that the

Disciples did not ask Jesus, "Lord, teach us how to pray." They said, "Lord, teach us to pray". The point is this. We learn how to pray by praying. It is not a theoretical or ivory tower thing to study the intricacies of it. Prayer is something to do. You learn how as you do it. Lord, teach us to pray!

What do you do when you pray? Worship God with all your heart. Bow, jump, dance, sing, raise your hands, lose all your inhibitions and praise the Lord. I like to praise God for 30 minutes or more without interruption, listening to praise music and singing aloud to Him. Worship God as you proclaim His attributes, character and deeds. Focus on the Lord and praise Him. Also, ask God to manifest Himself in the lives of others. Pray for your friends, family, ministries, churches, missions, countries, leaders, etc. God listens and answers. Pray for God's will to be done and His kingdom to come. Remember "aim small, miss small"? Well, pray small. I mean, pray specific and precise prayers.

I cannot emphasize enough how powerful prayer is. That is why Satan tries to keep us from doing it. He is content with us reading our Bibles and going to church. He doesn't mind us knowing theology or having good friends. But when we pray, the kingdom of darkness is under attack and he hates it.

My pastor used to say, "Prayer is worship. Prayer is warfare. Prayer is work." It is hard to pray because we have to crucify our flesh and because many times we simply do not see results, especially if we are praying for spiritual things, for other countries, for missionaries, etc. It is also hard to pray because it is indeed warfare, and Satan attacks us when we pray. He distracts and attacks. Whatever he can do to make us stop.

Make a set time each day and pray for 30 minutes or more. Communicate with God. Speak to Him, listen to Him, tell Him your heart, your fears, your desires. Worship Him. Experience Him. Pray.

SERVE, NOT JUST ATTEND, A CHURCH

Imagine a professional football player on the Tampa Bay Buccaneers. He is paid a lot of money. He is talented. He is vital to the team's success. There is only one problem. He doesn't play. He suits up and attends the games. He doesn't play. He says, "I am on the team. I attend practice and the game. That is good enough." Is it? Is he really a professional player if he does not play?

Read the title of this chapter again. I am emphasizing your role. It is easy to attend a church and think you did your job. The player goes to the game. Attending a church is good. It is Biblical and beneficial. If all you do is attend, it is harmful.

What do I mean by that? It is harmful because it substitutes something good for something great. God has designed us with community in mind and attending a church does not accomplish community. He illustrates it with our bodies. Our body has many members, many parts, but it is one body. Here is what we think. We look at church and if we just go, our assumption is that we are not hurting anything. This is true. Going to church doesn't hurt anyone, but who does it help? In your body, let's say you break your first two fingers, and they have to be taped. After the first few days, they do not hurt anymore. The pain is gone. But now, even if they are not hurting, are they helping the body? Try zipping your pants, brushing your teeth, or buttoning your shirt with your fingers splinted. They don't hurt, but they are not helping and their lack of helping is hurtful. You have to try to compensate for what they should have been doing. There is no pain, but there is a problem.

God designed us to help the local church. The church needs you. God put you there because of your gifts, talents, and abilities. The church needs you to minister and bless others. If you don't, it may not 'hurt', but the goal of life is not to avoid being hurt. If you don't serve, then you are not helping. Others must compensate for what you are not doing. The body is hurt, not because you are causing it pain, but because you are not helping it.

Serving in a church is beneficial because it blesses others. It also blesses you in a couple of ways.

First, it is more blessed to give than receive. This applies to serving with your time, talent and spiritual gifts and your money. You serve Jesus as you serve His local body, the church. A second blessing is it makes you accountable and responsible. Sometimes as a pastor, someone would come to me upset because they had left the church, oh say two months ago, and no one had contacted them or even knew they left. This is not a pastor problem, or an issue with the church. If these people could miss 8 weeks of church and not be missed, the problem was them. They did not serve the body, so no one noticed their absence. You are accountable to the people you serve. You cannot miss because they depend upon you. If you have a moment where you "Don't feel like going", you go anyway because others need you.

When you find a church, from day one, jump in. Volunteer for a weekly ministry. Become part of the a/v team, the setup crew, the worship team, or a Sunday school teacher. Get a job that requires you to be there every Sunday. Be the type of person who, if you are gone, there is a hole everyone can feel, and few can fill.

Jesus said the greatest person is the biggest servant. In seminars I illustrate this by drawing a typical organizational triangle on a board and say most of us want to be at the top of the triangle with a lot of people below us. God turns the triangle over. Then go one step farther. I draw the image of a tree in the inverted triangle. God wants us to be the roots. That is the part that provides nutrients, stability and strength so the tree can have fruit. This is what you want to do in a church. You want to become a leader, which means a servant. As you do that, then God uses you to change the lives of others, and their eternity as well. Seek to provide stability, strength, help, and growth to the church.

There is nothing wrong with looking for a church that can serve you and meet your needs. You need them as much as they need you. However, once you find a church that blesses you, then you bless it! Be the tide that lifts up every boat in the harbor. Make sure because of your life, your ministry, your gifts and your talents, God blesses the church through your life. The church is the body of Christ. The church is the bride of Christ. The church has been given the keys to the kingdom and promised the ability to defeat hell itself. This is a community you want and need to be a part of; and more than that, it is a community that needs you to be a part of it.

SATAN IS REAL
AND HATES YOU

In our culture, we have a genre of movies called Horror. We did not let you watch them and we do not watch them. They focus on the power of the demonic. It amazes me Christians enjoy them.

I am more amazed by this. People who watch horror movies think more often about the demonic than Christians. We never think about the reality of Satan. I mean, right now, how often have you actually thought there really is a literal devil and he truly has millions of lesser demons to do his will? How often do you ascribe demonic activity and influence to the things in life? How often do we pray for protection or deliverance, or even consider we or someone we love may be under attack? Rarely, if ever.

In 1996 I became depressed. It was the first and only time. I felt like I was in a funk. I just wasn't happy. I was sad. I was depressed with nothing depressing in my life. I was sad, when my life was awesome. I went to see my mentor, a SBC pastor named Rick Ferguson. I told him I was depressed and the fact I had nothing to be depressed about made it even more depressing. My personal life, family life and professional life were great. Yet, I was depressed.

"Do you think it might be demonic?" He asked. "Maybe the enemy is seeking to get you to focus on yourself. I am not saying it is, but it could be."

I never considered the option. I fasted and prayed and asked God to deliver me from oppression if it was a spiritual attack.

I woke up after my fast. The depression left. I am convinced it was spiritual. We live as if there were no devil. We think that the biggest problem we have is some decision we need to make about money or time. The devil is real. Satan is alive. He is not a boogey man. He is a literal evil personified. He is real. He hates you and wants to destroy you. He wants to devour you. He wants to ruin you. He has one goal. He desires your utter and total pain and annihilation.

What would you do, if you were at home one night and some-one broke into the house? They were armed with a large knife, and they were a sociopath. They had one goal. They wanted to kill you after they hurt you. They wanted to slice you to death and let you drown in your own blood. They wanted to murder and destroy you. What would you do if this were not a movie, but a reality? Someone was in the house and they wanted to kill you!

I imagine you would look for a way to escape them. I would think you would find some type of weapon to fight them if needed.

I was 15 years old and at home by myself one night. I walked to the bathroom and on the way back to my bed, I saw someone was in the house. This was before 911 and we lived in the country. A robber was in the house with me. I got my arrows and put my razor hunting tip on them. I knew I might have to defend myself.

In Colorado one morning, around 2:30, a man started trying to break in the door. He knew we were home. He was high on some drug and sought to rob us. I went upstairs and got the baseball bat. I put all of you in a locked room. Mom had al-ready called the police. I yelled down to him, "We called the police and they are on the way. If you come in the house and stay downstairs, I will leave you alone. I am upstairs with my wife and children. If you come upstairs, I am armed and I will stop you." I knew there was an enemy threatening my family and I would die for them. Isn't that what you would do if some-one was really in your house and really wanted to kill you? You would try to escape but be ready to fight?

Satan is in the world. He is in your arena of life. In your house. He is really here. He is armed, more than dangerous, and wants to kill you. It is a fact. It is a reality. It is a truth. Now, what are you going to do?

The Bible teaches us to watch out for Satan. How do we do this?

First, acknowledge that he is real, and he is more powerful than you. If I was there, and I had a gun, and you knew someone was in the house with a knife, would you try to fight them with a sandal or wake me and my gun up? Satan is real, and he can kill you. He can easily destroy you. He can wipe you from the face of the earth. You have no chance against him. That is why you must learn to depend upon Christ and live in His presence and with His power. As soon as you realize you are up against a temptation, go to the most powerful weapon in the universe. Go to the Presence and Power of God.

The second thing to do is to try to get away. If you knew the bad guy with the knife was in the living room, and you could get away by running through the back door, then run. Remember the knife fight I told you I was in when I was in High School? A guy pulled a knife on me. I ran like the wind. There was no fight. I have no stitches, did not get cut, and am still alive today. I told my friends if I ever got cut in a knife fight it would be in my back because that is all the person will see. I got away. You want to get away from Satan, which means getting away from his temptations.

In our family we say, "The best way to avoid sin is to avoid temptation." Learn to stay away from things which tempt you. These are the weapons of Satan, and he is using them to destroy you. Recognize them for what they are. If you know you are tempted in some arena of life, then for goodness' sake stay out of it. Get away from the things the devil can use to tempt you.

When you are tempted, run away from Satan and to God. Really, do that backwards. Run to God, which will take you away from the temptation. Pray out loud. Quote Scripture out loud.

verbal

For example, you are with your boyfriend or girlfriend and you kiss. You become sexually aroused. Stop. Quote the Bible out loud and then ask God to give you the strength to overcome this temptation and live pure lives that honor Him. Then go home. You bring the power of God into the situation, apply the word of God to what is happening, and then run like the wind. From now on, do not allow yourself to be alone in a place where sex could happen. The best way to avoid sin is to avoid temptation. If you are never where you could have sex, then you won't have it.

Satan wants to destroy you. He will use sin, temptation, impurity, bad influences, and your own heart to do so. Sin is not a little thing, no more than a little uranium in your coke is. Put a drop of Uranium in your coke and what happens? Radiation sickness kills you in six months. Put a little sin in your life and it will kill you. You may not taste it now, or see it, or even truly realize that it is there, but it will kill you. It will destroy your life.

Satan is real. Sin is real. Satan will use sin to ruin you. Avoid both by running to Jesus!

REACH THE WORLD

I share this story in my book, Discipleship of the Heart. I was driving home from work one day. I worked in construction on apartment complexes while attending university at night. Suddenly, a car pulled up beside me and the man inside started waving me over. He wanted me to stop on the side of the interstate. At first, I thought it might be road rage. However, I had done nothing. I was driving my junker car in the far-right lane. If he were upset over my top speed of 45, he could easily pass me. I looked at him and the look on his face was not one of anger. I sensed no threat. I pulled over.

He jumped out of his car and yelled, "Joe! It is you!" I had no idea who he was. "Do you remember me?" He asked.

"I am embarrassed to admit that I do not. You look vaguely familiar, but not really. Who are you?" I asked.

"I am not surprised you don't remember me. I will never forget you." He spoke. "Last year I worked with you. I only worked one day. After seeing how hard it was to do the job, I decided to find another one. At lunch, you shared Jesus with me. I told you I wasn't interested and did not believe. We had a nice talk. I did not get saved. One thing happened. I could not get the gospel and the love of Christ out of my mind. I could not forget what you said. It kept coming back into my thoughts. Anyway, I want you to know, I got saved three months ago. I prayed and asked God to let me tell you thanks. Here you are! Joe, thank you for telling me about Jesus!"

That was one of the best conversations I ever had. It was such a joy. I lived on that high for probably a month. I did not remember him or our conversation. I shared Jesus with all of my coworkers on a regular basis. He is such a part of my life. I have to talk about Him. It is an overflow. It is so easy. Yet, I have found that one of the easiest things to do has been somehow transformed to one of the hardest things to do in the church. We have relegated the purpose of our existence on earth to an option for our lives. I truly believe it is an act of spiritual warfare and we have been defeated, temporarily, by it.

I am talking about sharing the gospel. It is our call. It is our privilege. It should be our passion.

Whenever you meet someone, two things happen. You formulate a first impression of them, and they make one about you. Many times, our first impressions are wrong, but they are the most lasting impressions. Because of this, we want to be slow to make judgments about others, but we also want to be proactive in the judgment they form about us. We want their first impression to be as accurate as possible.

This is one of the reasons I believe you should let someone know, from the very beginning, you are a serious follower of Jesus Christ. They need to understand if they need help from a godly person; you are the one to go to. Let them know you are serious about loving Jesus and you interact with God. Be the example of Christ to them. Let them know they can expect nothing less than integrity and honesty from you.

Just be real. A real follower of Christ. Here is what happens when you do this. First of all, many temptations will be avoided because radical sinners will not want a Jesus lover at the beer fest, and people looking for sexual partners don't want to sleep with a lover of God. So, you will avoid many temptations.

A second thing is it immediately identifies you as the spiritual expert, and therefore the person to go to for help in times of trouble. This will give you a lot of opportunities to minister to others.

Third, it makes you accountable. You are not a secret service Christian. They know who you represent, so you must live up to it. You will avoid some temptations, and then because others know you a Christian, you will have power to overcome others.

So, from the start, let it be known who you are. For example, when you are interviewing for a job: "Let me tell you about me. I am child son of an evangelical pastor and missionary, and I lived on the mission field in Bolivia for 12 years. I am a devout Christian. This means to you, as an employer, I will not only work hard, but I will also not come to work drunk or on drugs. I won't miss due to a party the night before my shift. I will not lie to you and I will not steal from you." You can easily talk to people about our faith and how you lived on the mission field. Segue into your own declaration of faith. You can invite people to church and church activities just like you would invite them to the movies. You can turn down invitations. For example, "I am sorry, I can't go on Sunday because I participate in the programs of my church. Can we do it another day?"

Let people know, as soon as you can, that you love and follow Jesus. Identify with Him, not with a peer group. If someone is looking for Jesus, let them see Him in your life.

The next aspect moves from living your faith to speaking it. Your faith, your life, no matter how devout and holy you are, will save no one. Salvation comes from trusting the life, death and resurrection of Jesus. Use your relationships as quickly as possible to speak to your co-workers and friends about Christ. Our definition of evangelism is: Sharing the story of the Son, in the power of the Spirit, leaving the results to the Father. You have done that with us. We went door to door sharing Christ more than once. You have seen me do it at our outreach programs and you did it with me. Now you are on your own. You are not my child serving with me in the ministry. You are not my child evangelizing with Papi. You are God's child seeking to make His Son known. Do it. Nothing is more important than your family, friends, co-workers, classmates and neighbors knowing Jesus. Live out your faith in front of them and share the faith with them.

The final thing is to always engage in missions. Missions is the heartbeat of God. His mission is to reach the world He loves. He wants to change lives, help the poor, and transform souls. He does this incredible and eternal work through you.

Find missionaries to give your money to and give them a lot of money. Give money to projects and campaigns. Take short-term trips every year if possible. If God did not call you to go, He called you to send. Support missions through prayer, encouragement and money. Look at us. We are missionaries. We support five other missionaries in three countries. Each month we send them $100. They need support and we need to give. Pray daily for missions and missionaries. Read their newsletters and respond to them. When missionaries are in town, take them out to eat, loan them your car, buy them a gift. Love, support and be a part of what they are doing, and through that what God is doing in the world. You can give. You can pray. You can go on short-term trips. You can send people on short-term trips. You can encourage, send emails, write letters, mail gifts...whatever. Just make sure that every week missions are a part of your life. When you are engaged in missions, you are a part of the work of God.

WORK HARD

I have worked a lot in my life. I had to work in order to eat. My family was poor. My siblings and I all had jobs by the time we were 14. We had to work. I went through school debt free. Through the university and graduate school, I worked on the assembly line at General Motors 60 hours a week, had a part-time job and was on staff at a church. I did this as I took a full load of 15+ hours in school. I have done jobs from telemarketing, driving, factory, and construction. I have worked in offices and in the rain. I have been blue and white collar. One thing I noticed in all the jobs I did. People who work hard are hard to find. This skill, this activity, this character trait will truly separate you from the pack. The Bible says we are to do everything to the glory of God. We are to work in such a manner as to please the Lord. Our goal is not to get the praise of man, but the pleasure of the Lord as we work.

Most people don't work hard. They go to work. They do their job, but they only do that. They just do what they have to do in order to get finished and/or paid. They meet the requirements of the job. It is a rare person who seeks to do more than he/she has to do. It is even more rare to have an employee try to excel at their job. "Work is a four-letter word". We hate our jobs. We work for the weekend and dread the weekend ending because that means work starts.

The goal of many people is to retire. It is not just to retire. It is to retire early. We want to stop working as soon as we can. One time a co-worker shared with us her cousin had actually won $1 million dollars in the Texas State Lottery. She was so happy. The word she used to describe it was 'good'. More than once she said, "It is good she won it." I took the conversation deeper and asked her what she meant by the word 'good'. Did she think it was morally better to have a lot of money than to be poor? Did she think her cousin would now be a better person because they had money? What was 'good'? Her answer was now her cousin would not have to work anymore. Her cousin was a single woman of about 30 years of age. She could retire and spend the rest of her life not working. No one in the conversation at the break table thought someone might want to work. Work was an evil this person no longer needed to encounter.

Why is it we think work is bad and non-work is good? Why is it we think that loving to work is weird? Whatever the reason, people do not work hard. We do not try to be the best we can be at whatever task we are presented with. Unfortunately, the idea is the nail that sticks its head up gets hammered. We have a tendency to shrink or rise to the norm. When I worked at General Motors, my boss told me I worked too hard. I bothered the other employees with my work ethic. I did too much and exceeded my job description. I was told that I was making others look bad and have to work harder. At General Motors they have a phrase that the management uses when they are serious and need to be obeyed. The supervisor says, "This is a direct order." When they say that, the employee can call their union representative, but in the meantime they must obey. On two occasions I had supervisors tell me, "Joe, I hate saying this, but this is a direct order. Stop working so hard." The reason was I was working and doing all I could the best I could. I did things not in my job description. I repaired items I saw were done poorly. I picked up trash. The other people were upset because I did too much.

God made us to work. He created Adam and gave him a job as a caretaker of the world. We are to be like Jesus, Who said, "My Father works and therefore I work". Work is a virtue. Work is a good, moral activity. It has become a four-letter word and most people 'hate' their job. This isn't because of the job. It is the heart of the person. We work in order to have money to play. Work is seen as a bad means to a good end. The entire culture daydreams and fantasizes about winning the lottery and being able to stop working. The idea is that work is a necessary evil to be avoided if possible. This isn't true. Work is good. We should work because it is a good thing to do. Enjoyment of your job doesn't come from your job. It comes from being 'In-Joy' while you work. Joy is a fruit of the Holy Spirit. Work is not simply to provide us with money to spend. It is also a means to meet the needs of our family and others, to make relationships with those who need Christ, and to develop character and responsibility within us. Learn to see work as a morally good part of your life.

Now that is a perspective on work. On to the how-to. It is simple. You are not there to check off time and get your hours in. You are there to help your co-workers, serve your boss, and make your company more successful. Your goal is to represent Christ in the workplace, with all of His virtues, and to serve others. Simply put, do the most you can the best you can. Things like starting time. If starting time is 8, you be there no later than 7:45. If quitting time is 5, never stop before 5:15 unless forced to by a time clock. If you see something that needs to be done, do it. (sounds like our house rule, doesn't it?). Don't define your job by what you have to do. Do everything that you can do in order to serve those around you. Don't wait to be asked and don't seek credit. Simply learn what the company, your crew, whatever does and do as much of it as you can. One great thing about this is it is makes an impressive statement about you to others—and therefore about Christians—and therefore Christ. Another good thing is it makes time go by a lot faster. Activity has a way of putting us into a time warp. You work and forget about how long you have been there or how long you have to go. A watched pot takes forever to boil, and clock-watching makes 8 hours into 12. Just show up and start working until someone tells you to quit. A third thing is, and this doesn't always happen, but if you have a wise or business minded boss, hard work gets rewarded. I think a good rule of thumb is that if you are not tired at the end of your shift; you didn't work.

We have had a statement on the wall of the living room. It

states: "I will do everything to the best of my ability and to the glory of God." That is the principle to apply.

Now, let me move out of the workplace and into your relational life. Work hard. So many people put effort into making money, but none into making friends. They try to get promoted at work, but never promote their family. As a pastor, I once had a man who ran a company of leadership come to sell me his product. He told me it focused on how to determine your vision and mission, then to set action plans and goals to move the church or organization into the direction and finally attain the plan. He emphasized having and adhering to a value statement. As I got to know him over lunch, I discovered he had been a pastor, but had left the pastorate after his divorce. Now, I do not know any details, and am not throwing down a blanket judgement, however I bet he did not apply the principles he knew to be true for work in his home. In your relationships, apply the same principles you do to be successful in the career field. Plan the work and work the plan. Set goals, plan activities, develop others. God has given you these people in this moment of time because HE wants to WORK through you to help them become better. Once more, look to our example. From discipleship time with you, to saving money for large purchases and vacations, to playing games and going places...Mom and I have been intentional in our relationship with you. We have had a goal—for you to love Jesus Christ with all your heart. We have tried to do things—work—to make that goal a reality. In your relationships, do the best you can to the glory of God.

How about school? Work hard. This means that you put the energy into the activities that you must do in order to be successful. Your goal is not to pass the class, nor is it to get an A. Your goal is to learn the material, to understand the principles, to evaluate them considering Scripture and apply what you can to your life. It is to become a better person because of this class. Work in your class. Work on your projects. Work on your studies. Work on your notes. Work on your tests. Do school to the best of your ability and the glory of God. The same principles apply. Plan, think, set goals, look ahead, do the tasks, and pay the price. All of this is part of working.

Your spiritual life. Work hard. Do the tasks you need to do in order to accomplish the goals you have. God works in and through us, and only by constant dependence upon the Holy Spirit can we bear fruit as we abide in Christ. However, we can do things as the Holy Spirit leads us to cultivate it. These are the spiritual disciplines God leads you to do, and also, like your job, doing things you see need to be done. Items as simple as avoiding places of temptation, keeping your heart pure, meditating in the Word, memorizing Scripture, sharing your faith, and serving a church. These are the nuts and bolts. They are not the purpose, but they are a means of working towards the purpose of knowing God better, loving Him more, and bearing spiritual fruit.

Working, in my opinion, and I believe the teaching of the Bible, is to be a constant part of our lives. That is why we need the Sabbath. Work doesn't stop at the workplace. We work from sun up to sun down. We work in our studies, homes, families, and relationships. Work hard in every area of your life. Work, scientifically defined, is focused activity. That is what we are to do.

SET AND AIM
FOR GOALS

Growing up in Latin America gave you guys a love for soccer. You love to play it. You love to watch it. I like the fun we have watching the World Cup, the Olympics of soccer. The average game takes 90 minutes and ends with a score of 1-0. The players spend the entire time running an average of seven miles, to try and kick the ball into the net. They have a goal. They have a purpose. They train to get the ball into the other goal.

All sports have a goal. There is a target. The teams have a purpose.

Remember going to the shooting range? We spent two hours trying to hit a target at various distances. We knew success. It was when we hit the target in the correct spot. Failure was the opposite.

It seems like we have goals everywhere except our lives. Every time you drive, you have a destination in mind. A goal pulling you towards it. What about in your life? What is pulling you?

I teach this at my pastor's conferences. I get a volunteer on the stage and give a ball to them. Then we just stand there.

"Come on. We do not have all day. Finish the illustration." I tell them. They do not have a clue about my expectations. I keep heckling them. Finally, I point at a trashcan I set up before the session and a piece of tape on the floor. "Stand on the tape and make the ball go into the can." The tape is close, so they almost always succeed. I finish my introduction with this. "I gave him the tools he needed to succeed. He had the ball. The problem is, he did not know what success meant. He did not know the goal. He wanted to use the ball but did not know the target. Once I explained how to use his giftedness and he saw the target, he could succeed. We do this in our lives and our churches. God gifts us with our abilities, passions, spiritual gifts, education, etc. He gifts our members as well. We all stand around doing nothing because no one has a goal. No one knows what to do. We cannot measure success since we do not know what success is."

You need to have goals in life. You should be proactive in living. If you are not proactive, you are reactive. Someone is determining the direction of your life. Is it you? Or is it someone else?

Always have a direction to your life. Know where you are going and why you are heading that way. A great way to do this is to always have written goals. I heard a news clip about a research project a college did. They discovered the top 5% of the Forbes 500 executives all had one thing in common. They all wrote and aimed for personal growth goals.

Your mother and I have marriage goals, couple goals, and personal goals. We have financial goals and spiritual goals. These are written down and looked at.

That last sentence is important. A goal is not a goal unless it is in writing so you and/or others can see it. It is just an idea until you put it on paper. You articulate better on paper. You see exactly what it is you hope to accomplish. Let me give you some ideas on how to do this.

First of all, write out in one complete sentence what your goal is. The sentence should be as concise as possible while fully stating the desired outcome. This means you thought through the goal enough to summarize it. One sentence smaller than a tweet.

Ask yourself why you want this goal. The Bible tells us to let God examine our hearts and our motivations. Does God speak to this, or to the attitudes behind it? Is there a principle in the Bible about this? The main thing here is to make sure your heart is pure and good. For example, if I have a financial goal of a certain amount of money, or a tangible goal such as a car, I need to ask myself why I want these things. Am I greedy? Am I coveting? Am I becoming a lover of money? Am I being a wise steward? Am I seeking to purchase something I need? Ask God to check your heart.

A great exercise is to ask yourself why you have not already reached this goal. If it is important to you, why is it still in the future? What are the obstacles, problems or distractions which have prevented you from this? Have you just not tried? Is this a brand-new desire?

If you know exactly what you want, and you have examined your heart, then give the goal a deadline. A goal without a date is nothing more than a dream. A deadline makes it real. Your goals should be difficult to attain, but with hard work and discipline do-able, and you should be able to do it by a particular date. Don't say, "I am going to get a bachelor's degree." Instead, state, "I will finish my undergraduate studies with a bachelor's degree in Business by December 2022." This not only makes the goal specific, it also gives you a finish line to cross. You will know if you are successful or not on that date.

Break the goal down into steps. Imagine you have a goal of taking a photo at the statue of El Cristo on your birthday at noon. How are you going to get to the statue? You want to walk there. So, you take the stairs. The way to El Cristo is one step at a time. You cannot just 'be' there. You have to get there. That is how it is with goals. Using the goal in the paragraph above, "I will finish my undergraduate studies with a bachelor's degree in Business by December 2022." I can now develop a plan. What steps do I need to take? If I have to have 120 hours of credit to get that degree, then I should have 60 hours by December 2020. What classes do I need to take? In what order do I take them? How many hours per semester? How much money will it take? How can I get the money? Where will I get my degree from? When do I have to register? These steps start with a definite goal and then working backwards.

Develop your plan using each step and giving it a date to accomplish. I start from the end and work backwards. I imagine myself with the goal accomplished and then start asking what had to happen for this to take place? I write down every task that I can think of and then put them in chronological order. A great example is in building. Builders use a project plan, not just a blueprint. The blueprints and the final concept are the goal. The project plan gives us the steps in order to accomplish it. I have to do the work on the site before I can roof the building. I have to put the pipes in underground before I paint the walls. I have to frame the building after I pour the concrete. When I pour the concrete, I have to wait a certain amount of time for it to dry before building on it. The walls have to be able to hold the weight of the roof. They think every step out. It would be hard to put in the electrical cables at the end of the job. They have to do in before you sheetrock and paint. In your tasks, look at the order you need to do them. For example, in your degree plan you cannot take English 3301 until after 1301 and 2301. There are prerequisites. What are the prerequisites to each task in your goal? When I moved to Colorado to start the church there, I had written over 300 individual tasks I had to complete. My goal said, "My church will have its first service in thirteen weeks with over 100 people in attendance." I worked backwards and put these tasks in order and gave each task a date. We had our first service 13 weeks after moving to Denver and had over 130 people.

Evaluate your progress constantly and make adjustments as necessary. You do not want to move your deadline or change the goal. The evaluation determines areas to work harder or faster in order to achieve the goal. I want to finish my undergraduate studies with a bachelor's degree in Business by December 2022. I realize that at the end of 2020 I only have 45 hours of credit. Don't change the goal to December 2023. Instead, take enough hours in 2021 to close the deficit.

Only change your goals if God leads you to or life circumstances change. We can not know the future. We can make our plans, but the Lord directs our steps. I was going to pastor a church in Texas. I had one and two-year goals written. I was on track. God intervened and led me to start a church in Denver. Later, I thought I would live my life and ministry out in Virginia. We had family, financial and personal goals with this in mind. God called us to Bolivia. Be willing to do what the Holy Spirit and the Word leads you to do. Your goals are your servants, not your master.

EVALUATE YOUR LIFE BY FRUIT

One benefit of life in Bolivia is we eat healthy. Fruit is a huge part of our diet. When all ten kiddos lived with us, we purchased seventy-five pounds of fruit a week. Imagine you are there right now. You can see the huge fruit basket on the table. I hold up a banana. What type of tree did it come from? Okay, now a mango. What tree supplied this fruit? I can do this for the berries and the vegetables after the fruit. I know, without a doubt, you can tell me what plant gave which fruit. A banana tree grows bananas.

So, let me ask you a different set of questions. You see an angry man. What is in his heart? There is a greedy man. What is in his heart? You know a person addicted to sex. What is in their heart? Look at how patient that person is. What is in their heart? Did you hear how kind the person in front of you spoke to the barista? What is in their heart? You can tell the type of tree by the fruit it bears. You can tell the type of heart by the fruit it bears.

We constantly look at what we do to determine who we are, or how good we are doing. We do this in the educational and professional realm. We also do this in the spiritual. The problem is God doesn't evaluate us by our legalistic devotion to actions. He tells us to look at our fruit. Our fruit reveals to us and others the depth and sincerity of our devotion to Christ. Our fruit reveals our maturity.

Go to Galatians 5, Philippians 1, James 3 and other passages and see if these virtues, these fruits, are the knee-jerk reaction of your life. If you shake a fruit tree, or a vine, the fruit that falls off of it was on it to begin with. The fruit that falls to the ground when something bumps the tree tells you what kind of tree you bumped. Are you patient, gentle, kind, loving, humble, meek, and joyful? When someone wrongs you, what is your heart and thought response? That reveals your heart. If you see evil fruit fall out of your mouth or into your mind, it gives an opportunity to run to Calvary. Jesus died for you because of this sin in your heart. His death and resurrection can transform you into a better person. Evaluating your life by the fruit of your life allows us to check our hearts for the presence of sin or the power of God. At any given moment, our fruit reveals our dependence. Am I depending on God or myself? It reveals our purpose, to honor God or promote self. It reveals our passion, God or self. The spiritual disciplines, and/or other activities, only reveal what we are willing to do. Spiritual fruit is who we are and want to be.

The following is a long excerpt from "Discipleship of the Heart". It teaches this, so why reinvent the wheel? I also don't have to worry about plagiarism.

This is important. This is another life-changing truth. I came across this over 20 years ago. I was studying spiritual fruit, and something happened. I realized how central fruit is to the Christian life. I took time and looked at every verse in the Bible which mentioned the word fruit. I looked at every passage that mentioned 'a' fruit. I read every single place God used the word love. I did the same thing for all the other listed fruits. I took a pink highlighter and went through my study Bible, and every time God mentioned a spiritual fruit, I marked it. The amount of pink highlighter surprised me. I studied the purpose of fruit.

In the Bible, fruit does three things, and those same three things happen in our lives today. Fruit reveals to us the tree it came from. Fruit reproduces life. It also gives nourishment to others. This is the same thing that Spiritual Fruit does in our lives. We can see the truth about who we are by the fruit our lives manifest. Our lives are to bring other people into the Kingdom and spur them towards maturity. This describes the reproduction of fruit. The final thing is that we are to be a blessing to other people. These are the purposes of fruit.

I discovered fruit is the standard by which God measures our growth. We like to use other things. We use things such as church attendance, quiet times, Bible reading, doctrinal knowledge and/or the use of our spiritual gifts. We evaluate our lives by how much we read the Bible, pray, go to church and try to get other people to read their Bibles, pray and go to church. We like to use these things because they are safe, and we have control over them. If good doctrine is how I am evaluated and how I evaluate others, I can study and read. If church attendance is the standard, I can go to church. If morality is what we are looking for, then I can make sure my life looks good on the outside.

Fruit is not like that. Fruit is not something we control, it is something that God does in us, and it is what God uses to determine whether we are growing in Him. As I taught in the section on love, I cannot love others unconditionally. I am incapable of this feat. Therefore, if unconditional love is the evaluator of my life, I will either be a failure, or I must depend on God to help me. Fruit is what God measures us by because fruit reveals who we really are and how much we are abiding in Him.

I looked up the fruits individually, and then the word fruit itself in the Bible. For example, God uses the word love 880 times and the word goodness 802 times. The Bible uses the word fruit, and the actual fruits of the Holy Spirit, 4,499 times. A quiet time is never mentioned in the Bible. The Bible doesn't tell us to read a few verses and then pray for five minutes every morning. However, God uses the word fruit 4,499 times. This is serious to God! If fruit is so vital to the Christian life, we need to understand what it is.

Fruit is who we really are. I can try to deceive you and myself by acting like someone else, but my fruit reveals the truth. In the story I told in the previous chapter, I was pretending to be a good Christian pastor and father. My son could see by my fruit of anger and hostility that I was not who I was pretending to be.

It is by my fruit that I can know myself. We love to emphasize in our culture that we should not judge other people. I am not saying you can judge me, although you can, according to the Bible. I can judge myself. I may think I am a great Christian man. My fruit reveals the truth.

I love to illustrate this when I am teaching it by embarrassing a teenager. Here is what I do. While preaching, I pretend that my voice is a little strained. I find a teenager in the crowd and point to my water glass that I left on the front row. I ask them to bring it to me. As they hand it to me, I drop it so it spills all over the floor, on the stage, in front of everyone. This happens with a lot of smiling and laughter:

Joe: Oh my goodness! Look at that! Dude! Why is there water on the floor?

Teen: Because you dropped the cup?

Joe: No, that is not why. Also, you dropped the cup, don't blame me. Why is there water on the floor?

Teen: Because it spilled.

Joe: No. Why is there water on the floor?

This continues to the frustration of the teenager until I stop and say, "There is water on the floor because there was water in the cup. If there would have been coffee in the cup, then there would be coffee on the floor. If there would have been juice in the cup, then there would be juice on the floor. There is water on the floor because there was water in the cup. What is in you is what comes out when you are bumped."

As the teen sits down to the grateful applause of the audience, I continue to point this truth out and apply it to our lives. We love to focus on the outside and make our cups appear good. However, what spills out when we are bumped is what was inside all the time.

At this point, I hold up my Bible. Unknown to the listeners, I have a tube of opened toothpaste inside of it. I show them the Bible and talk about how nice it is, the leather cover, and that it is God's word. This is our lives. We seek to appear good, and we contain (know) God's word. But what happens when our children disobey? What happens when a driver cuts us off in traffic? What happens when a co-worker does not deliver on their responsibility? What happens when my spouse is mean to me? What happens when the opposing political party member does something that I disagree with? What happens when life squeezes me? I squeeze the Bible, and to their surprise a long gooey stream of toothpaste oozed out of it. Every time that I have done this, there has been an audible expression of grossness such as "Uuugggh".

I ask them what it is and pretty quickly someone identifies toothpaste. Now, no one knew that it was inside the Bible. It was not until the Bible was squeezed that what was hidden inside became visible for all of us to see.

That is how Spiritual fruit works. My fruit is the knee-jerk reaction that I have to life. It is what falls from my branches when I am bumped. It is not the pretty decorated mug that I carry around. It is what spills out of that beautiful mug when I drop it. At this point, I put three identical cups on a table. One cup is full of water. The other cup is full of coffee. The last cup has orange juice. I ask them which cup has which liquid. We talk about it some and then even vote. I hold up one cup and then pretend to get bumped by someone and I spill some contents.

As soon as that happens, I then ask again, "What is inside of this cup?" Everyone knows the answer because they saw the contents of the cup when I was bumped, and they spilled out. I repeat this with all three cups. I then finish by putting the cups on the table but hiding the order. I ask again, "Based on appearance, what is in this cup?" No one knows since they all look identical. It is not until they are bumped and the liquid spills out that we can know what was inside.

When something bumps me, the thing that comes out is what was inside. I can know my life and my walk with Christ by what comes out when I am bumped. It may not be visible to others, but I can see it. It is my knee-jerk reaction. It may not be what I do, it is what I want to do. For example, a wife is snippy to her husband. His internal and immediate reaction is that he wants to put her in her place. He wants to be argumentative in return. He wants to one-up her comment with a great retort and put down. However, he has learned that if he does this, the marital spat is not worth the pleasure of the remark and he probably won't have sex tonight. So, he does not do it. He either says nothing or says something to try to smooth over the situation.

The fact that he wanted to it reveals his heart. He was not kind to his wife. He was selfish. He did not put her down because he is like Jesus. He chose to not argue because he wants to have sex. His fruit, that only he saw, is anger, malice, and selfishness. Other people saw a conflict diffused by a patient man. It was all an act. It was a conflict avoided by a selfish man who did not want to endure the consequences of revealing his heart to others.

Fruit reveals who I am. The reason that I am a grumpy and gripey person at home and not one at work is not because my wife and children are worse than my co-workers to be around. It is because I have learned I can be mean at home without real retaliation. I change my behavior and hide my character at work. At home, I allow my fruit to reveal who I am. I am a grumpy and mean person.

My children were in the kitchen one day, and one kid accidentally hurt another one by stepping on their bare toe. The hurt child, an eight-year-old, yelled in anger at their sibling and tried to push them.

I intervened and asked, "Why did you yell at your brother?"

My son responded, "He stepped on my toe."

"Yes", I said, "He stepped on your toe. But why did you yell at him?".

My son thought for a moment and said, "I yelled at him because in my heart there is anger, and when he stepped on my toe, it came out."

I told him he was correct, and it was why he needed the grace of God. He was the type of person who would yell and violently respond to a slight pain caused accidentally by his brother. He needed the gospel to become better than that. There was no punishment. My purpose was not to change his behavior, so he learned to muffle his angry response. My goal was to help him take that angry response to the cross and have Jesus exchange it for patience.

Can you see how incredibly profound this truth is, and can you imagine how much life would change if we would live it out? This little eight-year-old child already knew that the only way for anger to come out of him was if anger was in him. Nothing actually makes me angry. However, there are many things God can use to reveal the anger of my heart. Fruit reveals who we are to ourselves and to others, but let's focus on ourselves.

I came home and my wife had a horrible day. We have 11 children, and my wife is a homeschooling mother. This means her life is consumed with the trials of full time parenting multiple age kids. So, I came home, and she had a trying day. A short time after I am home, she speaks unkindly to me. Instantly I think to myself, "You cannot treat me that way. I have done nothing wrong. It is not my fault you don't make the kids obey, nor that the house is dirty. That is on you. You don't speak to me like that. I am your husband. I...."

The Holy Spirit convicts me. I realize what has happened. My wife bumped my branches and judgment, hostility, self-righteousness, and anger fell from the tree. So, I pray, "Dear Lord, I need You right now. I just realized that my heart is in sin. The things I wanted to say to Denise are not from your lips. Jesus, You died for me because I am the type of man who would be mean to a woman who has sacrificed all of her own desires for the good of my family and love of me. I see my fruit, and it is not pretty. Would you forgive me, fill me with your Spirit, and allow me to speak love to my wife?"

My fruit revealed to me my need for Jesus. I responded to it and He answered my prayer, allowing me to be gracious and loving to my wife. This is how fruit reveals who we truly are to us. Many times, probably over 100 in the years we have been in ministry, people have complimented my wife on how patient and kind she is. They have said that they can see it in how she treats the children, me and others. I had the children make a film for Mother's Day this year and in it they complimented her. Three of them mentioned how patient and gentle she is with them. Denise doesn't even know it. She doesn't try to be patient. She has not taken a life development course on kindness. It is the fruit of the Holy Spirit in her life. When she is bumped, patience, kindness and gentleness fall from the branches. She is this because of God.

Fruit reveals who we are to ourselves. It is also a measure of personal character growth. This is self-explanatory, but if I am angry when bumped, but over time in which I constantly repent and seek forgiveness I see that I am gentle when bumped, I know that I have grown a little more like Jesus.

In 2 Peter that as God describes our growth, it is almost all fruit. I believe these, even knowledge is the fruit of the Holy Spirit because the knowledge that this is speaking of is the knowledge of God based upon context. Even if it is not, self-control, perseverance, kindness and love are mentioned. Then God's desire that we will not be 'unfruitful'. This goes back to the beginning of this chapter where I pointed out that we love to measure our spiritual growth by other metrics. Instead of evaluating my life by gentleness, peace and goodness, I like to point out that I can defend my particular view of election. I know my eschatology and I have a firm opinion on women in ministry. We have made our growth standard to be an increase in academic knowledge. How much do we know? It is amazing how we so many times our standard or focus has become the opposite of what the Bible teaches. Read the last part of 1 Corinthians 8:1, Knowledge makes arrogant, but love edifies. We focus on what we know and because of that we become arrogant. God says that love is the key, not knowledge, love, which is a fruit of the Holy Spirit. The Bible says that it is not our knowledge or actions that reveal our heart. It is our fruit.

We also see spiritual fruit in our evangelistic endeavors. It is not only in the physical world we see that the purpose of fruit is to reproduce the life of the tree, but the Bible also alludes to it in the spiritual world. If you do not have spiritual offspring, you really do not have fruit.

I mentioned in an earlier part that the metric of our lives is to glorify God. Here is an activity that I have done several times with pastors. I ask them what is the purpose of our ministry and our lives? I then gently lead them to the answer, "We are to glorify God."

I will ask them to tell me how to glorify God. The answers are all generic ones centered on religious activity. From direct praise and worship to attending church and reading our Bibles, I am giving a list that could be narrowed down to: Read your Bible, pray, go to church and try to get other people to....

It is amazing to me that God has told us in His word in direct terms with no room for misunderstanding how to glorify Him, yet I am never given that answer. Look back at John 15:8.

My Father is glorified by this, that you bear much fruit, and so prove to be My disciples. (John. 15.8)

If the goal of my life and the reason for my very existence is to glorify God and the way I glorify God is to bear much fruit, I should focus my life on bearing His fruit. God chose us to be part of His spiritual orchard. He is the Husbandman, and we are His vineyard. People like to argue over election and predestination. I do not want to argue over how but look clearly at the what. God chose us in order to bear His fruit. He did not elect us for heaven. He elected us for fruit. If we are not doing this, then we are not living in the written will of God.

Fruit is the Holy Spirit producing in me, and reproducing through me, the character and kingdom of God.

Fruit is the Holy Spirit...this is vital. We do not produce fruit. Fruit is not the result of a Bible study or small group event. It is not anything that we can do in our flesh. It is the by-product of our yielding to and being filled with the Holy Spirit. In the next chapter I will talk about the moment by moment walk, the abiding factor, of the Christian life. When we do this, abide in and be filled with the Holy Spirit, He produces the fruit in us. The illustration Jesus used in John 15 is classic. If you cut a branch off of a tree and throw it on the ground, it will not grow fruit. A branch does not grow fruit unless it is connected to the tree or the vine. The life of the vine flows into the branch, and fruit is the result.

Fruit is the Holy Spirit producing in me...God is at work in my life. I can see what He is doing as I see the fruit in my life. If you look back at all the spiritual fruits itemized in the Scripture, you discover that they reflect character growth and life change. God is at work in me.

Fruit is the Holy Spirit producing in me and reproducing through me...God does not bless me so I will be blessed. He blesses me so I can be a blessing. One of the most important aspects of fruit is reproduction. God is not only at work in my life, He is at work through my life. God uses me. That results in my life affecting the lives of others. A great example of this is the teaching on His love. He gives me His love in order for me to love other people with it. I am blessed to be a blessing. I am not a reservoir where God's blessings are stored like the city water supply. I am a river of life where God's blessings flow to and through me to give life to others downstream.

Fruit is the Holy Spirit producing in me and reproducing through me the character...this is the obvious reading of the fruit. Moment by moment I am being transformed into the image of Christ. The Holy Spirit is conforming me to the image of Jesus Christ by producing the life of Christ in me through fruit. I am becoming like Him, not in my appearance, but in my character and bearing. I am adding moral excellence to my faith. As I disciple, mentor and train others to depend upon Christ and walk in the Holy Spirit, I am helping others in their own character growth. As I teach people to listen to the Holy Spirit and respond to Him, I am allowing God to not just produce in me, but reproduce through me, the character of Christ.

Fruit is the Holy Spirit producing in me, and reproducing through me, the character and kingdom of God....this last aspect deals with evangelism, missions and ministry in the church. God is at work, not just in my life and through my life, but by using me and my life in His church and His mission in the world. As I grow to be more like Christ, my passion will be what His is...world evangelism and discipleship. My goal is to bring all of my life under the reign and rule of the Father and to help others do the same.

You need to look at your fruit. Make it a moment-by-moment habit and response to life. What do you see when you get bumped? When your life is shaken? That is your fruit. If it does not glorify Christ, go to calvary.

FOLLOW THE FLOW

I shared my faith with a college student last year. He typified today's youth. His standard of truth was no standard of truth. He believed truth is relative to the situation. He used the phrase, "My truth" or "Your truth" a few times. The more we talked, the more obvious a foundational chasm existed. Postmodern culture has reversed the normal flow of truth. Here is what we do in our culture.

Behavior—Belief—Truth.

Let me explain. We start off with a behavior. The most obvious one is homosexuality. Due to the influence of Satan through entertainment avenues, homosexuality is pervasive in society. The gay lobby did an awesome job of using the courts to change culture after they failed in congress. As Dave Chappelle calls them, "The Alphabet People", now have a powerful presence in society. Every news story contains something about transgender, gay, lesbian, bisexual, etc. As I write this, President Biden's Equality Act passed the House and is in the Senate. It makes sexual orientation into a civil right. There are very few people who will still say that homosexuality is a sinful choice. Our cultural shift declares it wrong to say something is wrong. It will tolerate no one who does not tolerate. I can declare homosexuality a normal lifestyle but cannot declare heterosexuality as the normal lifestyle. All of us know a gay or lesbian person. In television series and movies, the gay or lesbian is the most likable character. Our gay friends are great people. How can someone say Archie is a sinner and going to hell? He is the nicest guy I know. I never met a Christian better than Archie. He loves his husband and child. He is moral and upstanding. He is a policeman and active in the community.

I share this with you to show what happens.

There is a behavior participated in by people. This behavior becomes widespread in my peer group or the culture. Something this pervasive in society must not be wrong. We move from behavior to belief. We believe the behavior is good, or at least not bad. They base the Equality Act on a belief. People believe biology determines sexual orientation instead of morality. It does not take long to move to the next port in the flow.

We declare what we believe to be truth. As of this moment, if someone states homosexuality is a sinful choice, we treat them as close-minded bigots. You must not understand science. Sexual orientation is in our DNA. A person does not choose their ethnicity, or their orientation. This is not science. They do not prove it in any form. We declare it truth. Now, if I stand against homosexuality, I am fighting truth.

We move from behavior to belief to truth. Look at the average white evangelical church. Based upon appearances and spending choices, it would appear we believe greed is a virtue. We behave in a covetous manner. We spend more and more money on material things and seek material wealth. We now call it financial freedom and stewardship. The prosperity gospel has owned the hypocrisy. They declare it truth. The 'truth' is God desires us to be healthy and wealthy. Orthodox evangelical churches are still at the belief stage. We behave as if we were covetous, greedy, envious and jealous lovers of money. We 'believe' it is stewardship to accumulate wealth. Our behavior changed our belief to eliminate the disconnect.

The correct order is to discover truth. Do not use cognitive bias. Seek truth. We established our ultimate authority is the Bible. Therefore, discover what the Bible teaches. Once I know truth, I make the choice to believe it. In my homosexuality example, I will be honest with you. Homosexuals, lesbians, gays, etc., do not bother me. I am not abhorred by the behavior. I am not disgusted. I like them. Seth had a lot of gay and lesbian friends. I bought them dinner. If I believed homosexuality was not a sin, I would put the same effort in their equality as we do equality for minorities. The issue I must do is this. I discover God's perspective. I refuse to believe the lie of Satan and think I can determine good and evil. God does that. He teaches in His Word that homosexuality is a moral choice. It is a sinful action. It is wrong. I now have to believe His Word, or no longer hold to it as my ultimate authority. I believe Him. He states the Truth. I go from Truth to Belief.

The next stage is like Paul said, "I believe therefore I speak." I move from belief to behavior. Since this it true and I believe it, I act on it. Pornography is a sin. God teaches us this in His Word. It is sinful to lust. I believe Him. I therefore refuse to view pornography in any form. I run from it. I will not do it. I will not lust after any woman. Truth molded belief that dictates behavior.

God teaches me to be generous. His Word shows greed and coveting to be sin. I learn the desire to get wealthy is wrong and the deceitfulness of riches can choke my spiritual life. The truth is I should give a lot of money to world evangelism and meeting the needs of others. That is the truth. I believe it. I believe the truth of God about money. That belief dictates behavior. The truth is generosity is good. I believe that truth. Therefore, I give away a large percentage of my income.

Truth—Belief—Behavior

This is the flow. God put His Truth in His Word. Discover the Truth. Believe the Truth. Behave according to the Truth.

MAKE WISE CHOICES

I was about to graduate seminary and ready to pursue God's call on my life. I suddenly found myself at a crossroads. I was not at a crossroads of two paths. I had four exceptional opportunities in front of me. I had to choose what to do from these four. All four choices were great. I would love to do any one of them. My problem was which one of the 'love to do' would I pick. I did not know what God wanted. I did not know what to do. My wife said she would honor and trust my decision. I prayed. I fasted. I prayed more. I fasted more. I simply could not see an obvious winner or clear loser. This scenario has played itself out several other times in my life. What do we do when every choice is good? I go back to what I learned at the moment of my first choice. I rephrased the question. I asked myself a question which has given me a compass to live by since. Andy Stanley, in his book, "The Best Question Ever", shares his own story and discovery of this question and how it applies to life. I recommend that book as it took my question and made it even more in depth.

The lives we lead are and will be the culmination of the choices we have made. If we make good choices for the most part, we will receive good results. If we make bad choices, we will receive bad results. The key to having a wonderful life, therefore, is simple. It is to make good choices.

Wisdom is not an option for success, it is the road to success. Over 450 times in the Bible, God uses either the word 'wise' or the word 'wisdom'. In the Proverbs, God even personifies Himself as wisdom.

One thing that happen as we mature is that we have the blessing/burden of hindsight. We look back at our lives and we can see there are relationships we should have avoided. We own things we regret purchasing. We can look back and see morally wrong decisions. We can identify the paths that took us to destinations we never wanted to arrive.

How can you change this from hindsight to foresight?

Our lives are so full of decisions. We have to make them every day. We make choices, some of which are little. Others are life changing. Your choice of lunch today is not as important as your choice of a spouse. Your choice of socks is nowhere near as significant as your choice of career. Life is full of choices. Some of them have eternal significance. Others have little to no significance, such as which channel you watch, they are all equally trivial. What if there were a way to not only identify and prioritize our decisions, but to make great choices on the significant questions?

You can do that. The secret is to learn to make wise choices. The fact is, the better my decisions, the better my life. From the time you were little, you have heard us say over and over that we would rather leave you wisdom than wealth. Many times, throughout your life, we asked you, "Is this a wise choice?" Choices are the fabric of life.

There are a few things to know about choices. The first is that God has given us the ability to make choices, not determine consequences. Our choices determine their own consequences. I can make a choice. I have to accept the consequences of that choice. It is like a train. My choice is the engine, and the consequences are the train cars attached to it. If you are in Dallas, sitting at the entrance ramp to I-20, you can choose to go either east or west. It is your decision. You make the choice to go west. No matter how much you desire it, you will never arrive at Port Canaveral in Florida. Your choice to go west eliminated the option of an eastern destination.

Our lives are the summation of our choices. Everything said and done, we are who and what we chose to be and become. I did not become this way by heredity or environment. I became this person by choice. There are things in life that are out of our control. When mom and I announced to all of you kids we were moving to Bolivia, you did not have a choice. You had to go. We may not have the ability to choose, but we can choose how we respond. Therefore, people who come from identical backgrounds end up in totally different lives. My life differs completely from my siblings and most of my childhood friends. Why? It is because we have over the years made different choices.

The third truth is that you can a wise choice. You can meet every important decision that you face with wisdom. The choice to choose wisely is yours to make. So, let's look at how to make good choices.

Let me start off with a working definition of wisdom. I put this together from many years of Bible study and reading. I think it encapsulates wisdom.

Wisdom is the fruit of the Holy Spirit that allows us to see and respond to people and events from the perspective of God.

I think that every word in that definition matters. True wisdom is a fruit of the Holy Spirit. In the book of James, God compares human wisdom with "wisdom from above". That shows that true wisdom is from Him and not from our human reasoning. Another reason that I believe wisdom is a fruit of the Holy Spirit is this passage (James 4:13-18) not only parallels Galatians 5:19-23, but it lists many of the same fruits. James mentions the wisdom is from above, and then other spiritual fruits such as purity, peace, gentleness, and mercy. It also sums up by saying full of good fruits. A few verses before, He mentions the spiritual fruit of gentleness. God imparts true wisdom to us as we abide in Christ and full of the Holy Spirit. As the Holy Spirit fills us and produces His fruit in us, we will grow in our wisdom.

The Holy Spirit allows us to not only see but respond. Wisdom in the Bible is an action word. We see wisdom in our actions. In the same passage of James, God says we see our wisdom in our behavior and good deeds. Wisdom is different from knowledge. Knowledge can simply be something in our minds.

We know something. Wisdom finds an expression in life. I can know how to manage money. That is knowledge. If I am wise with my money, then I put my knowledge into action and apply it. I can know the Bible teaches me to forgive others. Wisdom is when I apply that knowledge and forgive them. If we are wise, we will see all of life from God's perspective. The relationships, opportunities and challenges of life are viewed from His perspective. We will understand what He thinks about our situation. Wisdom compels us to act on God's perspective. It is much like the flow. We discover truth, believe it and behave according to it. We discover wisdom, believe it is the right choice, and do it.

We base a wise decision upon God's word. God's word is wisdom. If I am to see and respond to people and events from the perspective of God, then I must know God's perspective. I find this in the Bible.

What do you do if the Bible does not directly address the decision in front of you? Here are some basic guidelines for you.

Examine your motivation. Sometimes the decision isn't addressed in the Bible, but the motivation behind it is there. God doesn't tell me if I should purchase a new car or not. I look at my heart and realize I want the car to boost my image and self-worth. I think it will impress others. I want to be better than my peers. I do not need a new car but I want the feeling it will give me. Those motivations are easy to find in Scripture. If you were considering moving to another state or job, ask yourself why you want to. What is it about the 'change' that is appealing to you and why? What emotions or motivations are behind the desire itself? I have talked to pastors who were looking at going to another church, and missionaries considering returning to their home state, only to find when they truly examined their heart motivation, they discovered they had selfish reasons. Going to another church or returning to your home country is not a sin. The issue was they wanted to do this out of anger and frustration. They said it was Spirit-led. After examining their motivation, they realized it was not.

Research the facts. This is easy to do with the internet. You want to make as informed a decision as you can. Remember when we were considering going to the mission field, we interviewed missionaries. We talked to ten different missionary families and asked them serious open-ended questions. After we decided to move to Bolivia, your mom and I flew to Cochabamba and spent a week just gathering information so we could make an intelligent and informed move. Before moving from Colorado to Virginia, we researched the area in which we were going to live. We called the previous pastor of the church I was replacing and asked him hard questions. When you are researching, as best as possible, avoid confirmation bias. Confirmation bias is when you have your mind made up and you simply look for data to justify your choice. Look at the pros and the cons of the various options. If you are looking at colleges, try to contact current students and ask them for information. The best way to get accurate facts is through personal experience. Therefore, look for people who are doing or have done what you are considering. This is a type of application of the Bible when it tells us that wisdom comes from a multitude of counselors.

Limit your options. The number of choices can overwhelm us. The first time that we returned to the States after being on the mission field for over three years, we walked into a Super Walmart in order to buy chips. There were 192 different chip options. We could not decide. Your mom cried because she was so overwhelmed. We asked someone else to pick a bag of chips for us! There were too many choices. If you are looking at universities to attend, have a filter to limit options. First, limit your choices to evangelical universities. A second limiting option could be geographical location. Add a third one based on student body size. The goal is to end up with several great options instead of a multitude of okay ones. We prayed about the mission field and concluded God wanted us in a city. We wanted to have a ministry of evangelism and discipleship. That eliminated areas who already had a large evangelical presence. The size of our family led us to choose an area safe for families. We chose our mission agency and used this grid to give us options and we ended up with three places instead of an entire world. We chose Cochabamba from those three options. One thing that we have learned from living overseas is that Americans hate to lose options. That is why there are 192 chip choices at Walmart. It does not matter. Limit your options in order to make any decision at all, let alone a wise one.

Make a choice and dive in. The purpose of this process is to make a choice. So, do it. Do your best to filter and discern. Then, choose a course of action. There are very few irreversible choices in life. I just went over this with Benjamin. He had three job offers and did not know which one to choose. I reminded him of the fact he could always get a different job if he ended up hating the one he chose. It was not a choice for the rest of his life. If you choose a job, or even a career and discover it is not what you want to be doing, then change. Pick another option. You have to start. So, choose something and do it with passion. Do not have any hesitation. Throw all you are into it. Give it the best possible chance it could have to be everything you wanted it to be.

Evaluate your choice. After a set time frame, evaluate the decision. Was it a wise choice? Is there something else you need to invest in to make this choice even better than it is? Use finding a church home as an example. Your motivation is pure because God has told us we need a church home. Research and limit your options. You want an evangelical church with good doctrine. You want a church that focuses on grace and love. Talk to pastors and church attendees about the church. Then make a choice and dive in. Get engaged in ministry and fellowship. Be a vital part of the church. Give to it. Serve it. After a year, evaluate how effective and fruitful your ministry is to the church and the church's ministry to you. Are you helping others grow to know and love God better? Is the church helping you grow? Are you satisfied with the past year? Is there something more that you should do? After you do serious evaluation, decide what to do for the next year.

Do it all again. You have another choice to make. You always have another choice. Make your choices wise ones.

LEARN, LEARN, LEARN

I finally tired of hearing it and approached it head on this Christmas. Our older kids judge us for parenting the younger ones differently. They say snide remarks. They show we love the girls more than them. At Christmas after a remark, I said. "Of course we parent differently! Think about it. I became a father thirty-two years ago. I did not know what to do. I learned a little. I learned more as the years passed. If I parent Mercy the same way I parented Seth, twenty years older than her, it can mean one of two things. Either I attained parenting perfection twenty years ago, or I am arrogant and refuse to change or grow. I parent differently because I know better now. I am a better husband than I was thirty-six years ago the day I got married. I am a better pastor, and do it differently, than I did in 1988 when I started the pastorate. I do my job as a missionary different from the day I arrived on the field in 2007. You saying I treat the younger kids different from I treated you is a complement, not the insult you mean it to be."

One of my life verses is in Haggai. God says the same thing in two verses. He says for us to "give careful thought to our ways." We are to love God with all our minds. Look at the Bible and see how many times it talks about knowledge, understanding, instruction, insight, wisdom and wise. I just looked up these words in the NASB and it uses them in 162 different verses. God tells us to seek these things out.

Be a learner. I don't mean get your education or your degree. You can have a degree and not be educated. All you have to do is pay the money, use your short-term memory, and jump through the academic hoops. Many educated people are not too smart, and even more are not wise. A learner means you are intentionally seeking to grow intellectually. You try to improve and develop skills. Here are some things that I recommend.

Develop a plan. I have a plan that incorporates reading, conferences, and classes. Last night, remember I am almost 58 years old, last night I started researching software development classes. I want to learn how to code. Your plan should be specific about books you will read, classes you will take, conferences you will attend, etc. If you don't plan to learn, you plan to remain ignorant.

Read. Read. Read some more. Since I was 18, I average reading two books a week. The past few years this slowed down because of life. I still read a lot and currently have 502 books on my kindle. Eighty percent of those are non-fiction. I have read over 150 books on marriage and parenting alone. Read books on leadership and work, and on personal interest. Read books on the Bible as well as the books of the Bible. Read books on finance, time management, and communication. Read about social studies and anthropology. Read science and history. Read, read, and then read some more. Reading a book for thirty minutes will do you more good in the short and long term than 40 hours of watching tv. So, just plan on reading a minimum of thirty minutes a day.

Take advantage of your classes. Don't just take the class, learn the material! If your goal is to make an 'A', you can do that without learning. However, if you thoroughly learn the material, you will also make an 'A'. You are in college. Take advantage of this and learn, even from the classes you have no interest in. Take advantage of podcasts. Go to conferences! In the States you can easily go to two or three conferences a year that will aide you in whatever you are doing. They are worth the price.

Be a learner. Lifelong and always. Learn.

PRIORITIZE YOUR CALENDAR AND LIVE YOUR VALUES

There is a famous either book or saying called the "Tyranny of the Urgent". The idea is we simply do screams at us to do, rather than what we know ought to do. I have taught and occasionally teach time management seminars. The best book I have ever read on this, and I encourage you to read it, is "First Things First". Most of us experience tremendous pressure and stress in our lives because we don't plan. The number one cause of stress is lack of planning and a close second is procrastination. We make our own problems. We have stress-filled lives because we know we neglect the important things. A pastor once told me, "I want to be a good father, but do not have time to invest in my children. That stresses me out." That illustrates this point. There are 'ought to' things in our lives. If we do not do them, we feel like a failure. We seem to not have time to do what we need to do. It is like with our money. The end of the month comes, and we have more month than money because we did not plan on how to spend it in advance. Therefore, we make a financial budget. A prioritized and thought-out calendar is merely a time budget. If we do not make a plan, we do the plan others make for us. Their plan will not reflect our values.

The key is to remember this: We don't manage our time. We manage ourselves. Time is not a commodity you can manipulate. It is not time you control, plan or administer. It is your activity. You control and manage what you do and when you do it. You are the key, not the clock. Now, take that one step further. According to Galatians 5, self-control is a fruit of the Holy Spirit, and if we walk in the Spirit, we will not do the things of the flesh. What am I saying? I don't manage time. I don't even manage me. The secret of time management (the misnomer) is to let God truly control my life. It is to do what He wants, when He wants.

Now, having said that to put our focus in the right place, there are principles we can do. I am going to put here a couple of things we talked about for you to remember by. The first is the life management chart that I designed. Let me illustrate with a story from "Seven Habits of Highly Effective People". I read this and since then used it myself in teaching. I taught a pastor's seminar on professional development and time management. I put a huge three-gallon glass jar on the table and then took some big rocks. I put the rocks in the jar until it was full and no more rocks would go in....about 8 of them. I asked, "Is the jar full?". The class replied it was. As the class watched, I took a bag of gravel and poured it in the jar. It went all around the rocks and then reached the top. Again, I asked, "Is the jar full?". The class said it was. I took a bag of sand and drizzled it into the jar, with it filling all the cracks surrounding the rocks and gravel. I asked, "Is the jar full?" The class was catching on and didn't say yes this time. I nodded to them as I took out a large pitcher of water and poured it in the jar. It surrounded the large rocks, the gravel and the sand. I asked the class if they knew the point of the illustration. The response was, "No matter how full you think your calendar is, you can always get more things into it." They were completely wrong. The point is this. If you had not put the big rocks in first, could you get them in jar now? In our lives, we have to decide what is important and plan on doing it before our calendars fill up with the non-important or less important things.

What are the big rocks in your life? What are the important things, the things you truly ought to do? Take these things and put them into your calendar before other things. It is like a dentist appointment. We put a dentist appointment on our calendar, and then for the next three weeks until the appointment, we schedule everything around that significant event. Identify what is truly important and then schedule it.

I have broken down my life into roles and responsibilities. Then, for each of these, I look at the coming week and month and ask myself what I need to do in order to accomplish specific goals in this role. I schedule the event. I put the big rock in the jar. One example is this book and our meetings together. You are a big rock. You are important to me. I want to invest into you and help you become an incredible person of God who loves Jesus and understand Biblical principles. That is WHAT I want to do, the question is HOW am I going to do it and WHEN will it happen? I took the goal of sending you into the world with wisdom and knowledge. Due to that goal, I wrote this letter. That is the same reason I chose to make this into a book. I meet with you and discuss these principles. Those meetings and this book is on my calendar. Now it is getting done, not just a 'wish I would have done'.

Start off and identify the important relationships, responsibilities, and roles God gave you. Look back over your values in the chapter on knowing yourself. I have identified my roles and relationships and other important values and then applied God's word to them. The driving passion is my life's mission statement.

"My purpose is to help people know God better and love Him more. I will do this by devoting myself to an ever-increasing knowledge and Spirit-filled passion for Christ. I will teach by word and deed that which I have learned and applied."

Every word of this is important and helps me define what I do with my life and in my relationships. It is to help people. The most important way to help people is to help them know God better. I want to use my life to bring people to Christ and to a deeper walk with Him. Knowing God is not the end. I want to help people love God more today than they did yesterday. We are to love God will all our hearts, soul, mind and strength. I want to help people love God. How can I do that? By devoting myself...by throwing all I am into an ever-increasing knowledge and Spirit-filled passion for Christ. I want to be Spirit-filled every moment. This phrase defines my life.

I want to become more like Christ, to live in the Spirit, and to love God more each day. I also want to help others do the same thing. Consider your life growing up in our home. You saw this daily. From personal evangelism, pastoring, and discipline others, to the way we sought to help you live by grace and listen to the Holy Spirit, all we did was to help you know God better and love Him more.

I identified the most important roles and relationships in my life. For each of these roles, a Bible verse reinforces the purpose of that role. These are my big rocks. Each Monday of the week, I look at the week and plan things to emphasize this aspect/role of my life. The first Monday of each month, I plan the month. The first week of January, and then again the first week of July, I go over the year and the remaining part of the year and plan different goals and plans for each role. I believe that there is a logical progression. I start with Purpose. I then look at the People in my life. I Prioritize Plans around the People and Purpose. The last is Production. It is what happens. Most people focus on production, and as a result lose sight of what really matters. It is the people in our lives that are important. Don't overlook people because you are trying to get things done. Purpose, People, Priorities, Plans and Production. In that order.

I will share my planner with you in order for you to see it and evaluate how you perceived me to live it out.

Role 1: Growing Disciple.

Bible Verse: "and you shall love the Lord your God with all your heart, and with all your soul, and with all your mind, and with all your strength." Mark 12:30

Purpose: I will pursue a continuing love relationship with the Lord Jesus by abiding in the Holy Spirit and participating in the spiritual disciplines.

Goal/Action Item: This is where I put a specific thing to do, whether it is fast, pray, read, memorize, meditate, etc.

Date/Time: I calendar the action item.

Role 2: Devoted husband

Bible Verse: "Husbands, love your wives, just as Christ also loved the church and gave Himself up for her" Ephesians 5.25

Purpose: I will show my wife that there is nothing nor anyone more important in my life than she is to me.

Goal/Action Item:

Date/Time:

Role 3: Loving Father.

Bible Verse: "Fathers, do not provoke your children to anger, but bring them up in the discipline and instruction of the Lord" Ephesians 6.4

Purpose: My children are a gift of God and the most important disciples that I will ever make. I will seek to instill a love and knowledge of God in their heart.

Goal/Action Item:

Date/Time:

Role 4: Missionary.

Bible Verse: "Go therefore and make disciples of all the nations, baptizing them in the name of the Father and the Son and the Holy Spirit, teaching them to observe all that I commanded you; and lo, I am with you [b]always, even to the end of the age." Matthew 28.19-20

Purpose: I will work with local churches and other missionaries to expand the kingdom of God through words and actions of love.

Goal/Action Item:

Date/Time:

Role 5: Author.

Bible Verse: "I am writing to you, little children, because your sins have been forgiven you for His name's sake. I am writing to you, fathers, because you know Him who has been from the beginning. I am writing to you, young men, because you have overcome the evil one. I have written to you, children, because you know the Father. I have written to you, fathers, because you know Him who has been from the beginning. I have written to you, young men, because you are strong, and the word of God abides in you, and you have overcome the evil one." 1 John 2:12-14

Purpose: I will seek to help people know God better and love Him more through writing articles, books and blogs.
Goal/Action Item:
Date/Time:

Role 6: Learner.
Bible Verse: "The beginning of wisdom is: Acquire wisdom; And with all your acquiring, get understanding." Proverbs 4.7
Purpose: I will never stop learning from others.
Goal/Action Item:
Date/Time:

Role 7: Administrator.
Bible Verse: "As each one has received a special gift, employ it in serving one another as good stewards of the manifold grace of God. Whoever speaks, is to do so as one who is speaking the utterances of God; whoever serves is to do so as one who is serving by the strength which God supplies; so that in all things God may be glorified through Jesus Christ, to whom belongs the glory and dominion forever and ever. Amen" 1 Peter 4.10-12

Purpose: I will do the necessary work and planning to maintain and grow my ministry and the kingdom of God.
Goal/Action Item:
Date/Time:

Look back at your life growing up. This is your first time to see my planner. You did not know I did it. Now you see it, can you understand choices I made? Except for the role as an author, a new role since 2020, I believe you can clearly see my attempt to live out my values. This makes life truly fulfilling because you do what is important to God and you, not what is important to other people. You control your life instead of surrendering control to others.

This is what I use to determine my big rocks and when I will put them in the jar. I advise you to make your own, with your own roles and responsibilities. Look at your passions and gifts and the people that God has placed in your life. Think about it like this. If you can allow God to control your time and your money, He pretty much controls you. That is the life you always wanted. One of the biggest causes of stress is we don't live out our values. We think something is important, but we do not do it. Prioritizing your purpose and your values allows you to pursue the life God has for you.

KNOW HOW TO COMMUNICATE

I plan to write an entire book on this subject, or at least have it as a large part of my book on marriage. The more that I counsel and help people, the more that I see the heart of conflict, and of conflict resolution, is the inability or ability to communicate.

Throughout our marriage, people have asked us what makes us so much in love and so happily married. There are several factors, but near the top of the list is communication. Your mother and I talk. You know that. We talk all the time. Your relationships will go no deeper than your communication can take them. Without serious, heart to heart communication, you will always have a shallow relationship.

When we first moved to South America and could not speak Spanish, we made so many mistakes. I took my motorcycle to the mechanic and asked him to repair my bacon. I tried to purchase a dog from a sports store when what I wanted a racquetball. The first wedding that I officiated I accidentally said, "In a marriage our joys are multiplied, and our penis is shared." I preached on Hebrews 12 about the great cloud of witnesses that surround us. Suffice it to say that in Spanish the word for witness is "testigo" and the word for testicle is "testículo".

We spoke one language, and they spoke another. It was up to us to learn their language because our goal was to communicate with them. We knew we had something of eternal importance to share. We had to share it in a way that they could understand. I could preach all day in English and no one would come to

Christ. They spoke Spanish. This is what we encounter in communication. Communication is not me talking. It is me talking so you can understand.

God not only created the ability and desire to communicate, He did so to us. Communication is so important God said that His Word is eternal and elevated above His very Name. When God named Himself, He called Himself "The Word". Think about that. God gave Himself a Name so that we could know and love Him. The Name given by the Godhead to the Son was, "The Word". Let that soak into your thoughts. Communication is of such vital importance to God His Name is Word. Then, God revealed Himself to us by revealing His written Word. In His Word, He allowed us to see Who He is and what He is like. He opened up His heart to us. We can know what God is thinking, what He is feeling, and what He desires because He revealed it to us in His Word. We know His mind and His heart. This is what communication truly encompasses. We need to do with each other what God has done with us.

This is my working definition of communication. I am not talking about just sharing small talk or niceties, even among family members. This is not the standard, "How was your day?", type of talk. That is fine. However, it will never take you to the deeper levels of relationship and understanding that true communication can. So, my definition of communication, based on what God has done and said, is this:

Two or more people going through the process of revealing to another what they are feeling and thinking in a manner that allows both participants to experience empathy and understanding.

Two or more people: Communication is not one person talking. In order for true communication to happen, you need both a talker/listener and a listener/talker. When one person is talking, the other(s) are actively listening to what is being said in order to understand it. They are not waiting for the talker to stop so they can talk. One person talks, the others listen. Then the other talks, while the first one proactively listens with a heart to understand.

Going through the process: It is a process. Communication and your ability to communicate grows as you do it. It is not a onetime event in which everything is said and done. In a relationship, communication must be a continual process that occurs day after day.

Of revealing to another: The only reason we can know and love God is HE chose to REVEAL HIMSELF to us. Apart from His specific revelation found in the Bible, we could never fully know or understand Him. He HAD to reveal Himself in order for us to know and love Him. This is the same in our relationships. Your mother can never know me unless I reveal myself to her. The Bible teaches no one knows what another person is thinking. The problem is we assume and then act on our assumptions. You must reveal yourself to me for me to know you. I cannot know you without it. I can only know the you I create in my imagination by assumptions and judgement calls. In communication, we choose to open ourselves up and reveal ourselves to another.

What they are thinking: The first aspect of self-revelation is I share with another my thoughts, opinions, convictions, ideas, etc. I don't rely on facial expressions to do what words were created to accomplish. I reveal to another what I think about whatever the topic is at hand.

What they are feeling: As we look at God, He did not just reveal His thoughts to us. He allows us to see His heart. We see emotions of the Deity in the Word. God let us know what makes Him happy and sad. He revealed His emotions. If you want a deep relationship, you must not just open up your mind. You must open up your heart.

In a manner that allows both participants to experience empathy and understanding: I don't just talk and tell you what I am feeling. The goal is for me to share with you in a way which allows you to empathize with me. Just like learning to speak Spanish, it is your responsibility to communicate in a manner the listener can relate to. I think this is one of the greatest problems in communication. We have replaced communication with talking. We talk and think we have communicated. If the listener did not fully understand me, I did not communicate.

I once saw in a conference on teaching, I cannot remember the name, in Hebrew the word for teach and the word for learn is the same word. The speaker said in the Hebraic mindset, if the student did not learn, the teacher did not teach. I love this. I use it in my teaching, preaching, and conferences. My goal is not to just disseminate information, or sometimes to verbally vomit on someone. My goal is to teach in such a way they understand and learn. This applies to communication in a relationship. The speaker enables the listener to understand heart and mind. If the listener does not understand, the speaker did not communicate. They merely talked.

There are a few more principles that can help you as you seek to deepen your ability to communicate. We find them in the book of Proverbs. Communication is one of the main themes in the book of Proverbs. Your mother and I practice this regularly.

As in most things, we need to start with the examination of our motivation. I need to ask myself why I feel the need to discuss this item. This is often overlooked. We do not struggle with our motivation; we worry about presentation. We go straight to 'how do I say it' and skip 'why do I want to say it?'.

This leads us to respond incorrectly to what God is doing. God brings things into our lives in order to help us see areas where we need to be conformed to Him. He allows us to experience things that reveal our hearts. Many times, the method of delivery is through our children, spouses, co-workers, roommates, and friends. He allows them to do something that bothers us, so that we see that we are the type of person who gets bothered.

Our response, unfortunately, is to look immediately at the messenger and neglect the message. God wants us to see our hearts, but our vision is obscured by the person giving us the insight. We fume over the other person instead of looking at why we are reacting this way.

When my motivation is pure, I want to talk so we can become more like Christ and I can glorify him in our relationship. If that is my motivation, my heart will be heard in my speech. People will listen to you when they know you want the best for them. This applies directly to my job as your Pastor. Do you know the most effective time of a pastor's ministry began after five years of ministry? It takes this long for people to know the heart of the pastor.

The next thing to do is to plan for a time to have the conversation. For many years, your mother and I planned 'Talk' dates. We scheduled a nice dinner. The purpose of the dinner was to address all issues in our relationship. This allowed us to pray in advance and to come to the event with a non-defensive and teachable spirit. A good rule of thumb is never start something that you cannot finish graciously. For example, do not start a conversation that may last for an hour or so at midnight. You want to be fresh and able to converse until you come to a mutually agreed upon finishing point. That point might be we need to talk more in the future, however you could advance the conversation constructively. Timing is vital. Don't walk in the house, drop a bomb, and then complain about fireworks.

Make an appointment together to block off time. Last week your mother and I met with the head of our church's mission committee. Something happened, and it hurt us. We contacted them and told them what happened and set up a dinner to talk about this event. We met and discussed it in love.

The last principle is to listen more than you talk and before you talk. You contacted them to communicate. Since this communication is before resolution, some of what you think and feel is based on assumptions and deductions. Make sure your point of view is accurate before defending it. Listening first might change your entire perspective.

Remember that the definition of communication includes both empathy and understanding. Therefore, you must think about what you are going to say and how you are going to say it. Your goal is not to just tell them what you are thinking and feeling. It is to help them empathize with you and understand your point of view. You need to be able to explain in a manner they can understand your motivation, doubts, fears, struggles, desires and goals. Think about the listener instead of what you are going to say. You must plan on saying it in the best possible way for them to relate. I have already used learning another language as the example. You must speak their language. Use stories and events to illustrate.

Choose your words carefully. Your tongue is a powerful weapon of destruction, or an incredible tool of construction. Speak in a non-offensive manner. Do not make accusations or heart judgments. Affirm the other person and reinforce the truth about your perception. You could be mistaken. Your assumptions might be wrong. Choose your adjectives precisely. Your goal is communication, not accusation.

Finish with both of you being able to restate the opinion and the feelings of the other person in your own words. Show you fully understand and are seeking to empathize. Bring it to a conclusion both people can express. What action items need to be taken, by whom and in what time frame? Do not leave the conversation assuming the other person knows your conclusions and that you know theirs. Express them. This is the absolute heart of all relationships. You must be able, and willing to communicate on an ever-deepening level.

HAVE A LOT OF FUN

I had a poor opinion of Christians as a child. It was not theological. I did not choose to become an atheist until High School. Even that was a moral choice disguised as intellectual. My issue with Christians was how boring they were. All the Christians I knew lived by a huge list of rules. My mom's church did not let girls wear pants. They preached against smoking and drinking. Movies were almost completely off limits. Rock-and-roll music was a sin. It seemed like Christians did not want anyone to enjoy life.

That is not an accurate image of us. I know now. I will say it still permeates the church. Many Christians are strict moralist who live in a constant fear of offending God. Others are so consumed with making a good life (materialistically), they do not have time for life.

The truth is God created fun. Laughter is a gift of God. Joy is a fruit of the Holy Spirit. God created us to enjoy Him and the life He gives. The word 'enjoy' sounds like 'in-joy'. :) The Bible says that God has given us all things for our enjoyment.

The happiest, most fun-loving people in the universe ought to be Christians. We have Christ in us and eternity ahead of us. We have the key to great loving relationships. If there is anyone that ought to enjoy life, it should be us!

When we first became parents, we established goals for you guys. We went on a weekend retreat and did an exercise where we imagined our last child turned 35 years old. All of our children were now adults. We asked ourselves what we wanted those adults to be able to do, and what we wanted them to be like in their character. Then we envisioned them talking to each other and remembering their childhood. What did we want them to say about growing up in our home and family? We listed those things. On that list was the word fun. We wanted all of you to have fun in our home. Think about how many times you have heard people say our family laughs a lot. That is because we do. You should too. Laugh at yourself. Laugh at life. Laugh at movies. Laugh at problems. Laugh with others. Become someone known for their jolly and cheerful attitude and a lover of life.

As much as you can possibly do so, live an adventure. We live on a budget. One of the largest line items in our budget is entertainment and vacations. Remember how we lived with 11 people in a 1200 sq.ft. apartment? We explained we were saving $400/month on our rental expense. We applied that $400/month to our vacation account so when we returned to States for our furlough, we would have a lot of money to spend on fun. We took two cruises and bought season passes to Walt Disney World. Mom and I went to Europe for two weeks. We went to the beach several times. We prioritized fun. We never purchased a car on credit nor had one less than 10 years old. Instead of buying cars, we took awesome vacations. Donors stopped supporting us because, "they could not afford to go to Disney". The reason they could not afford it is they prioritized a mansion to live in, and multiple new cars to drive. People spend their money on the newest smart phones and hottest technology. We spend ours on fun. Don't get tied to possessions that you cannot live. Life is an adventure, so live it to the fullest.

My income is less than most people. However, your mom and I have para-sailed and scuba dived. We went snow and water skiing. We climbed a 17,000 ft mountain and hiked into a canyon. We went deer hunting and sea fishing. We have done back flips off diving boards and jumped off of zip lines. We have done giant swings and rode every roller coaster we can. We went to Sea World, Disney World, Disneyland, Universal, Islands of Adventure and theme parks in Texas, Colorado, Virginia, New Jersey, South Carolina and Georgia. We have been to 18 different countries and taken 12 cruises. All of that on almost 50% of what most of my peers earn. That is because fun as a family is one of our highest values. We sacrifice other areas in order to prioritize this one.

We recommend you work for a few years and save up your money. Then, with a sibling or friend, go tour Europe for 3-6 months. Go to the greatest museums in the world and see the art for yourself, not just in a book. Tour the Roman Coliseum and see the Sistine Chapel. Spend all of your money and then come home and start life. You will never regret it.

Life is too short to not enjoy..

BE FINANCIALLY WISE

In 2006, we attended SIM's missionary training school. It was two weeks of extensive preparation. SIM required people to finish this training before going to the field. We provided financial information, including our debt as part of the class. At the end of the two weeks, I think over ninety percent of the applicants could not go to the mission field. They had too much debt. The mission required missionaries to be debt free, except for a mortgage and school debt. We could not have consumer debt and go to the field. We were in the small percentage of people allowed to go.

Back up even farther. In 1993 we moved to Colorado to plant a church. I took a seventy percent pay cut when I left the marketplace and entered the pastorate. The first year we lived in Colorado, we spent $500 a month from our savings account on our rent. In order to make our budget and fit my new income into our lifestyle, I fasted twice a week and mom fasted one day a week. We did not make enough money to feed everyone every day. On my thirtieth birthday, we went to Wendy's and split a 99-cent single burger. At the time, we had over $20,000 in our savings account. We did not touch it. Our savings account is not for living expenses. We moved to the ghetto in Denver in order to offset the $500 a month from our savings to pay rent. We found a duplex for $200 a month. This rent was $800 a month cheaper than the home in the suburbs. We now had a surplus.

This is the heart of financial wisdom. Spend less than you make. Live within your means. Save money.

We sought to instill financial wisdom in you. I told you we made written goals for our children. One goal is to raise financially wise stewards of God's money. We had you pay taxes from the money you earned, tithe, and set aside savings to teach you this. We tried to teach you money is a servant and not a master. Money is important. God talks a lot about money. Money, and if you add things that deal with money such as possessions, giving, gifts, ownership, envy, coveting, jealousy, greed, and theft, well it is probably one of the most talked about things in the Scripture.

The first thing to understand is that you do not manage money. You manage what you do with your money. You don't manage yourself, you let God manage your heart. It isn't my money that I am managing. I let God use me to do things with His money. The focus is not on your billfold; it is on your Savior. You need Christ to teach you and lead you in your finances.

In the American church greed and coveting are some of the most accepted sins. We build the entire culture of North America upon discontent and the desire for more. Madison Avenue marketers spend billions each year coming up with ways to get you discontented. We no longer preach against the desire to get rich. We do not take stands against greed or coveting. Everything in the American Church and culture is built upon the idea of bigger, better, faster and more. The problem is, it is never enough. Our career choices and our educational choices are driven by a desire to be rich. On multiple occasions I have been talking to seniors in high school. I asked about their plans. After hearing about what they want to do, I ask them why they want to do it. The answer ended up being the same every time. They want money. I never talked to anyone who wanted a low-paying job in order to focus on other things in their lives. The Bible says those who want to be rich fall into temptation, a snare, foolish and harmful desires. They might end up in ruin and destruction and even become apostates full of grief. You do not hear this preached in a church building a multi-million-dollar facility. In our culture it is hard to guard against greed, coveting, discontent, envy, jealousy and a love of money. Most of your co-workers, friends and Christian brothers do not share the value of simplicity and contentment. Guard your heart and your mind against the desire for bigger, better, faster and more.

Money is a something that God uses to examine our hearts and maintain our focus on Him. God allows us to have money, and also to not have money, to see if we are content in Him. He wants to see what we do with our money, because our money represents our lives. Our money is our life melted down and put in a coin form. The money I earned this week is the culmination of my education, my work experience, and my priorities. I see my heart in what I want to do with my money.

Money is used to meet my needs, the needs of others, and expand the Kingdom of God. God allows me to earn money so I can provide for my family, and my extended family. The Bible also teaches we can and should enjoy life, so one of those needs is the purchase of fun in all of its forms. My money is also how God meets the needs of the poor. God uses me to provide for those who cannot provide for themselves. God uses my money to expand His Kingdom and fund world missions. God blesses me financially so that He can bless others spiritually as I give to and through the church.

Money is also a treasure. It is to be saved and set aside to purchase items that have emotional, relational and social significance. The problem our culture has is this is the main focus of our money. Rather than use it to help others or expand the Kingdom of God, we simply want to buy more things. This is a part of money, but not the only part.

How do you handle your money? First, the most basic principle of all, is to spend less than you make. This seems like a no-brainer. This is such a basic principle, but the one that is violated throughout time and throughout the world. Almost no one in the west has an income problem. Money issues are 99.99% of the time centered on expenses. It isn't that we don't make money. It is that we spend more than we make and spend it faster than we make it. So, spend less than you make, period and always. In the section on fun, I point out to you how many exceptional experiences we have had as a family. The reason we can afford them is that since 1986 we have saved money every week out of every paycheck.

You need to have and use a written budget. I used two verbs in that sentence, and you need to do them both. You need to have a written budget. You need to use your written budget. A budget is to your finances what a day-timer is to your schedule. It is advance planning. Think of it as pre-planned expenditures. We don't mind pre-planned expenditures when we borrow money or use a credit card...we are saying today that next month we will do this with our money; pay a creditor. You use a budget to spend your money proactively in advance. Instead of getting to the end of the month and wondering where your money has gone, you start at the beginning of the month and say this is where my money will go. It is a roadmap of spending and saving. A budget is a prophecy of your money and a statement is history. The best type of financial freedom occurs when prophecy and history agree.

When you first start on your written budget, use the envelope system. It is so easy. Write out your budget, then make an envelope for each category. Cash your check and put the money in each envelope according to your budget. When the envelope is empty, you are out of money in that category and cannot spend anymore. For example, you put $100 in your entertainment envelope for the month. On the twenty-fifth of the month, you spend the last. Three days later, your friends want to go to a movie. You can't. You have no money for it. Don't transfer money, just make a note, and if you need to after a couple of months, you can amend your budget.

These two principles guarantee you financial freedom for the rest of your life. Live on a budget. Spend less than you make. Implement them and rejoice. You have seen the results of this in our lives. In 1986, we learned how to live on a budget with written financial goals. We lived on less than we earned. Since January of 1986, we have been debt free and spent less than we make. I keep reiterating this because I want you to know that we understand how hard it is to do, but that we have done it and it works. We made the sacrifices that we needed to make, and we continue to do so, in order to meet our giving and savings goals each month.

Now on to one other thing that we have talked about so much, but I want to put in writing. Remember, the price of an item is not how much it cost you. The price is the money you have to pay for that item. The cost is the money you had to earn in order to pay the price. The cost is considerably higher, because you allocate much of your money to other categories before it ever gets to your account. Take the price of the item and multiply it by 1.65. That gives you how much you need to earn to buy it. This is because you are wise, and you are giving to Christ, saving for the future, and paying your taxes. Example: You want to purchase an item on sell for $100. So, you have to earn $165 to buy it. $165-$16.50 (tithe) - $16.50 (long-term savings) - $33.00 (20% tax bracket) = $99 (or round up to the $100 you need). If you think when you earn $100 you can buy the item, you are wrong. If you do nothing besides pay your taxes and tithe, you are still $33 short of your goal. Now that you know this, evaluate the actual cost of things to see if they are worth it. If you see that the item actually cost you $165, and you only make $8/hour, then you are going to have to work 20 hours for it. Is it worth 20 hours? Evaluate things by their cost, not their price.

One more thing I have to say and stress with all my heart. You must avoid all consumer debt. Never under any circumstances incur consumer debt. The reason we use credit cards and/or finance things is because we are greedy, selfish, impatient, unwise, jealous, or coveting. It makes no sense to buy things you cannot afford. If you cannot pay for it right now in cash, you cannot afford it. A credit card will let you pretend you can afford it, but if you can't pay for it today, you cannot afford it. Avoid all consumer debt.

In your budget, have a line item for savings. We do not know what is going to happen in the future, however, applying the Biblical principle of decay in the universe, and the scientific principle of atrophy and thermodynamics, I can promise you this. Stuff is going to break. Your car is going to break down. You will have a wreck. Your phone will fall in the toilet. You will fracture your ankle on a curb, have a flat, or lose your wallet. A lot of unexpected and expensive things will happen to you. You cannot plan on exactly what, or when, but the guarantee is it will happen.

If you are living on a budget, you allocate your money to various expenses. Also, most likely when you first start out, you will spend practically all that you make, so when something happens you are in a pickle. Unless you have a savings account.

Here is what I recommend, and what your mom and I have done for over 30 years. Some things we save for are actually a part of our budget. We save for car maintenance (tires, tags, oil, repairs), and for vacations. We have a short-term savings account for things unforeseen. As part of your budget, put 10% in a long-term savings account that is not designated for anything. It is just an emergency fund you can use. Here is a real-life example. The first three months that we were in the States on our furlough in 2010, we had almost $10,000 in car repairs, home repairs, and unplanned travel expenses. None of this went on a credit card, and none of it was in a budgeted expense item. Where did we get $10,000? We have been saving and saving and saving. From before you were born, we have been saving at least 10%, and as much as 20% of our gross pay every month. This has given us a tighter budget to live on, but it has allowed us to be debt free, even when hit with a $10,000 whammy. This is why 11 of us lived in a 3-bedroom apartment. It is why we never drove new cars. We shop in La Cancha and before that at thrift stores. We put so much money in savings that we had to cut spending, but it is worth it in spades when you suddenly need it. Savings is a blessing. It starts off as a burden.

You should learn to live on less than you make after savings.

Save your money and spend nothing until you have no less than one year's worth of expenses in savings. If you do this, two things will occur. The first one is you will have no money to spend for a few years. It will still be painful. It is hard to live like you have no extra money.

The second thing that will happen is you will live for the rest of your life in total financial freedom, with no fear/worry about money. The freedom one year's expenses as a cushion gives you is incredible. If God calls you to do something, you can say 'Yes' immediately cuz you have no money problems or worries. You are debt free with bucks in the bank.

The third thing is that you will be able to respond quickly to the Holy Spirit as He leads you to meet the needs of others. You have the resources to bless others. I will talk about this in the next section on generosity.

BE GENEROUS.

This is a virtue and truth I learned by necessity. God gave your mom the spiritual gift of giving. Mom is generous due to growing up in the Watson's house. She saw the example of Paul and Darlene. The gift of giving multiplied this generosity. The first few years of our marriage, I struggled with greed. I desired wealth, and all it brings. We saved money, and it made me feel good. We saved money, and it gave mom more to give away. I knew and loved Jesus. I knew the Biblical teaching on stewardship. I understood generosity to a point. Mom was far more mature in the virtue of generosity than me. One day, she asked me if she could give all of our savings to a missionary. We were newly married, and it was a good amount of money to us. "If God leads you to, of course. You follow Him. I trust you." I said. Inside, it tore me apart. Finally, I told her, "If God leads you to give money, do it. Tell me about it after. I struggle so much with greed it is hard for me to joyfully give."

Since then, I learned the joy of giving and grew in the virtue. I also am passionate about giving because we depend on other people's loving donations to eat. We are now receivers and givers. It gives us a complete picture. We support missionaries and receive mission support. We know both sides. It is blessed to receive. It is more blessed to give.

God tells us in 2 Corinthians to grow in the virtue of giving. He equates the virtue of generosity with faith, knowledge and love. My initial plan was to include generosity as a sub point of the money chapter since it is key to financial freedom. The principle of generosity will bless you and others for eternity. It enables you to overcome greed, envy, jealousy, coveting and materialism.

This is the principle. Be a generous giver. Give. Give. Give. Give. Give generously. Give regularly. Give sacrificially. Giving to others is such a blessing. Think about how much Tim T. blesses our family. He gives us so many thoughtful gifts. He supports us generously. He also supports us thoughtfully. He is a great example of generous giving.

In the past, I taught people to tithe. I no longer teach it. I now teach generosity. I interpret the Scripture in a way which leads me to believe grace superseded the command of the tithe. I also believe the right perspective of money and a passionate love for God leads us to give generously. Generosity takes our focus on what we can accumulate and helps us look at who we can help. Historically, your mother and I give about 25-30% of our gross income away. The best that we have ever done is 60%. I hesitate to write this since I will publish this book, but I felt led by the Holy Spirit to include it to encourage everyone who reads this book. Giving generously is not only something that the rich can do. It is what all of us could and should do. On different occasions, your mother has given away all of our money. She emptied our bank account and gave the money to the Kingdom of God and we had to start over. That is awesome (and fearful).

I love the story of the widow's mite. You know it. The wealthy were all there at the donation box. They were showing off their large financial gifts. Everyone was in awe of how much they gave. Then, an old poor widow walked up and gave two cents. She gave two measly cents. No one was in awe of that poultry gift. No one except God! He was so impressed He inspired two of the gospel writers to include the story in their books. What was so important about two cents? It was a generous and sacrificial gift. It was all she had. She so loved God she gave Him everything.

We see the same thing in the Corinthians letter I referenced above. In chapter 8 we discover they were poor. Despite their poverty, they committed to give so sacrificially that the Apostle Paul asked them to reconsider. They begged him to let them give. Their commitment to God enabled them to give generously. Their focus on Him allowed them to consider the true value of money.

I urge you, my child, be a generous giver. Train yourself to give away a minimum of 10%. That is the starting point under the law. We are under grace. Grace results in a lifestyle of gratitude that causes us to do more than we have to do. I recommend you start at 15% of your income to the local church. You should designate a portion to go to world missions and evangelism. I believe that 5% is a good start. This means from the beginning and the rest of your life; you donate a minimum of 20% to the work of God. Always be open to the prompting of the Holy Spirit to give large amounts to needs He brings before you.

There are multiple blessings that come from this. One is the truth God said it is more blessed to give than to receive. When you obey God in your finances and give your money, it is not giving away your money it is investing your income. A return on investment, or ROI in the business world is based on two things: Interest and Time. You get a greater ROI if the interest rate is higher, and the same thing for the time. The formula is this: Principle (your investment) * Interest Rate * Time. $100 invested at 10%/year for one year means at the end of one year I will have $110. What does this mean? In the world, if you can get an ROI of 10%, then you are doing great. An average ROI is about 5%. A bank pays about 2%. God teaches us that when we give, we receive not 100%, but 1000% in return. That means that $100 invested for one year at 1000% would give me $1,000 at the end of one year. It gets better. God says that He will repay us at 1000% compounded, not annually, but eternally. Your spiritual investment has an infinite return. Your mother and I once met a missionary who was a church planter in the Philippines. He needed a van to carry himself and supplies to remote parts. The Holy Spirit led us to buy him a van. The ROI on our investment is this: we have a spiritual part of every soul who has come to Christ through his ministry. We invested in the kingdom, how much of a return is a forgiven and redeemed sinner? We helped start churches, fed the poor, and purchased supplies for those mountain and remote churches. Now and forever God will give us an ROI, that is significantly more than had we put the money for the van into a savings account.

Another return and blessing is God will use you to redistribute His resources to the world. He will view you as a water hose. He will bless you financially so you can bless others. You cannot out give God. For our entire marriage we have been giving, and we give a lot. Since coming to the mission field, we have received more than we gave part of our ROI. Now, every dime we receive is a part of our ROI for the past years of giving.

There is yet a third blessing to mention, and I am not talking about them all. I have already mentioned it in the opening paragraph. When you are a giver and not a taker, when you are a contributor and not a consumer, when you are seeking to be a blessing and not be blessed, it gives you such freedom. The cure for those evil temptations that surround money: greed, envy, jealousy, coveting, materialism, selfishness, pride...those sins are nipped in the bud when you become a generous giver. When you see money for what it is, and understand the eternal principles surrounding it, and live under the rule of the Kingdom of God, you are so free with your money. It is not your master; it is your servant.

Remember earlier I said to have fun? I mentioned some of what we have done. Those things cost money. I shared with you we budget a lot of money for fun. There is nothing wrong with this, but here is the difference. We are not doing these things because we are materialistic. We are doing them to have fun. Materialism is not part of our lives, grace giving uprooted it. I am not saying don't do things with your money, or don't buy things for yourself. What I am saying is generosity should characterize your life. This will only happen if you intentionally develop a plan for giving, and then as you follow that plan, listen and respond immediately to the Holy Spirit as He tells you to give more.

Be a sacrificial giver. Remember, a sacrifice hurts, that is why it is called a sacrifice. Give till it hurts, and then keep on giving till it feels good!

CHOOSE GOOD FRIENDS

There is a phrase repeated to me over and over in the ministry. Someone makes poor choices. They end up in jail or addiction. They ruin their lives. I ask their story. It starts off with, "I had a friend." The Bible warns us bad company will corrupt good character. The greatest influence in your life is friends. They help you be better, or they make you worse. They aide you in your spiritual and personal journey, or they hinder you. There is no neutral ground, friends are a moral steppingstone or a moral stumbling block. Your friends determine your values. They shape how you think and relate to Christ.

Usually, and this is why so many people get screwed up, we just let friendships happen. We become friends with the people at work or school. We become friends with people who have the same interest as we do or the same personality types. We just become friends, then we become like our friends. Your friends will be the most important influence in your life. They change you. God designed us this way. You cannot avoid it. Your friends are the most important influence in your life.

Friends are too important to let happen. Develop friendships based upon a common love of God before anything else. Pursue friends who love Jesus. Seek to be with people that are spiritual and holy. This is probably the greatest sacrifice we made on the mission field. You guys could not make deep and meaningful friendships. Our church did not have your age group and homeschooling limited engagement with others. You could not have school friends. Make your adult friends meaningful.

Be a part of a good college and singles group. If this necessitates driving to some large church or somewhere. Get your friends from church. Find other young adults who love God and want to honor Him. Remember your ring on your finger. The verse says, with those who call upon the Lord with a pure heart. You need a Godly 'those'. So, at school and at work you will meet people, know people, and like people. Get your friends from church. Try a lot of different church groups until you find one that has cool Christians loving Jesus and having fun. Then prioritize your work and school schedule around being with them. Do things with them. Invite them into your life. Go on trips, to concerts, and on mission trips. Spend time with them. I mean it. Your friends will have the greatest influence upon your life than any other thing. Choose your friends wisely!

CHOOSE YOUR SPOUSE WISELY

Mom and I have the greatest relationship on the planet. We are best friends. The working title of my book on marriage, don't let this gross you out, is "Having Sex With My Best Friend". (Eewwww).

Mom is my best friend. She is also my role model. I am her best friend and role model. She helps me be like Jesus. I help her be like Jesus. Our relationship grows us. I would rather be with your mom than any person in the world. We love each other. We like each other. We want to be with each other.

That is how it should be with your spouse. I said in the section on friends no one influences your life more than they do. It isn't totally accurate. Your spouse will be the number one instrument of God or Satan in your life. Okay, admonition and advice time. First the admonition. There is a tendency to become involved with others based upon their looks, and not their hearts or their walk with Christ. This is dangerous. You are soon going to 'fall' in love. You will start to love someone and the emotion of love clouds judgement. If you have relationships with a messed-up person, you will soon have a messed-up marriage and a messed up life. I am not saying that looks do not matter. They do. However, looks are not the end all. Looks are important, but do not let someone's good looks, witty smile or whatever determine the depth or even the beginning of a relationship. Looks can cause you to 'look' ☺. Look past the looks and see the person. Don't just date a good-looking person. Date a Godly good-looking person.

See the section on friends and magnify it 100 times, that is my advice on the opposite gender. Never pursue an ungodly person, and if one is after you run like the wind. You will date one of your friends. You will marry someone you date. If you have friends who do not improve your walk with Christ, you risk falling for someone who does not help you love Jesus. You will end up with a spouse who will destroy your joy and/or life. I am not overstating this. Your spouse is the single most important relationship outside of Jesus Christ. Jesus will change you for eternity, your spouse will change you in time. Your relationship with your spouse is the biggest blessing or greatest hurt in your life. You must choose one who blesses you. Do not choose one who will hurt you or is less than you.

Invest your time solely in passionate, devoted, and Godly Christian people. Do not flirt with others because it makes you feel good. Instead talk to, laugh with, be with, and date only the Godly. Your spouse, should in your opinion, be more like Christ than you are. Seek others who are passionately spiritual, engaged in their church, and pure physically. Be friends with, be with, serve with, and date only people whose lives reveal Jesus.

Back to your own heart and relationship with the Lord. The type of person who you want as a spouse will not be attracted to a spiritual midget or an ungodly person. Your life determines your spouse, and your partner will change your life. You have the looks, the charm and the talent to get a second glance from anyone, but have the heart and the spiritual maturity that causes people like Jesus to want to be around you. The more you are like Jesus, the more likely your wife will be spiritually mature and like Him. The more your life displays the spiritual fruit of God, the more likely your future spouse will bear fruit. Godly people want a Godly person. Be holy, humble, kind, giving, and good. Love Jesus, and the person who loves Jesus will be attracted to you. Bottom line is you want a spouse who is looking for a spouse who will help them become more like Christ.

IT IS MORE SPIRITUAL THAN YOU THINK

I know a missionary who shared this story with me. He traveled into mountain and remote villages. People realized he represented God. In one village they brought him an epileptic boy. The child suffered the type of seizures which caused total muscle spasms and loss of control. They asked the missionary to cast the demon out of the child. In another village, the story repeated with a blind person. They wanted the spirit of blindness cast out. The stories continue. Villagers blamed floods and bad weather, tornados and cysts on supernatural causes.

We hear these stories, and if you are like me, you feel sorry for the backward villagers. Epilepsy is an electrical malfunction in the brain. River blindness is a parasite carried by mosquitos. The weather is a natural phenomenon. Infections cause cysts.

The story gets even more confusing. The missionary agreed with the villagers!

That is so sad. How could Jesus be so backwards? Yes. The missionary I know is Jesus. The stories are true events from the Bible.

The difference between us and third world countries is straightforward. They see a demon behind every tree. We do not see the demon standing in front of us.

Ben and Kara went to a conference. I do not know who the presenter was. On their return, Kara told me one main point was this, "It is more spiritual than you think." I heard this phrase and it resonated with me.

It is more spiritual than you think. I do not think demons

cause all diseases. I do believe some are spiritual. The Bible says sin can cause sickness, even death. We see this in the effects and the cause. We see spiritual bondage and addiction destroy health. We know the consequences of sinful living. It is more than that.

We have had conversations about multiple personalities and other mental illnesses. How do we know these are not demonic possession? Serial killers and mass shooters often have no real reason for their kills.

The Bible plainly teaches there is another dimension. It is filled with supernatural beings. These beings can influence and attack the physical. Our only defense is a strong offense of prayer.

It is more spiritual than you think. For example, consider sex. We think of sex as a physical event. In Scripture, we see it is more than biology. It is a union of spirit. It is a mystery which represents Christ and the church. It is a moral choice. It is more spiritual than you think.

Your money management is not merely a way to choose how you will live life. It reveals your faith. It is a measurement of your commitment to the Kingdom of God. It shows you and others if you truly believe the Scriptural teaching of stewardship. It is more spiritual than you think.

I wrote to you about friendships. Friendships are not merely a physical relationship. They will help you be more like Jesus or less like Him. Your marriage is a picture of Christ and the church. We are called the bride of Christ. Our marriage is spiritual.

The disciplines show us how the body and spirit are intertwined. You cannot practice the spiritual disciplines without using your body. Your thoughts, words and actions are all physical with spiritual impact.

In the section on Satan, I shared my story of depression. In my case, it was a spiritual attack. A spiritual response handled it. It is more spiritual than you think.

We are not bodies with a spirit. We are spirits clothed in flesh.

These bodies are a temporary tent we wear. We are more spiritual than we think.

Look at life through the reality of the spiritual. Do not let western atheism and naturalism hide the supernatural. It is there. It is here. It is around us. Life is spiritual.

BE A RIVER NOT
A LAKE

I love the river. I used to drive to one near my house. In seminary, we studied the Nile River Valley. I learned the importance of the Nile to the Middle East. The study piqued my interest in rivers. Rivers flow and take life with them. Rivers are a source of life. The Nile is huge. It is the longest river in the world. It allows life where there could be no life.

I also like the lake. My only problem with a lake is it is just there. It is stagnant. A river might leave a lake, and it becomes dynamic. The lake itself is just a collection of water.

Be a river, not a lake. This means understand your purpose in this world and the Kingdom of God. You are here to carry life to others. You have heard me say, "We are not blessed so we can be blessed. We are blessed in order to be a blessing." That is a river. God pours His blessing into you. You carry that blessing to others. Mom's gift of giving is a wonderful example. God blesses her financially, and she blesses others financially. Blessed in order to be a blessing.

God gave you all of your abilities, spiritual gifts, money, time, and intellect. He placed you in our family to experience the life you have had. He did not give you all of this for just you. He gave them to you so you can pass it along. We receive from God in order to give for God. I mentioned a water hose in the chapter on generosity. It is a beautiful example. You are the hose. You connect to God, your source of life. He pours life into you. The life He gives you flow through you and into others. It brings life. We are blessed to be a blessing.

We see this in spiritual fruit. Fruit is not for us. I receive patience from God so that I can be patient with you. God gives me kindness because you need someone to be kind to you. You need to love. God gives me His love with your address on it.

Evangelism is the ultimate expression of this. I heard this once and took it as my own. God rescued us. We were dead and dying. He left heaven and rescued us. We could not save ourselves. We were hopeless and doomed and damned. The cross rescued us. Now, we have the ministry of reconciliation. God sends us into the world to tell others about Jesus. Listen to this. We are rescued people on a rescue mission. We are rescued people on a rescued mission. God did not just save me. He saved me to use me in the spreading of the gospel to save others. He rescued me in order to be a Spiritual First Responder. We are rescued people on a rescue mission.

Be a river, not a lake. Do not receive the blessings of God and hoard them. Bless others with them. God will bless you more. You can bless others more. A man asked me, "Do you believe the teaching of the prosperity people that says we give in order to get?" I answered him, "With one caveat. If we give in order to get in order to give, then yes. If I am the last link in the chain, no."

Be a river, not a lake. Let God use all of your life to give life to others. You are blessed in order to be a blessing. You are a rescued person on a rescue mission. Share your life.

LISTEN TO YOUR MAMA

This is so important.

Listen to me on this. I am not starting with some story to make the point. I am jumping into it. Your mama is the wisest and most Christ-like person I know. She is my role model and desires nothing but your success and blessing. She knows what she is talking about. She lives it.

If your mama gives you advice, listen to her.

If your mama admonishes you, listen to her.

If your mama encourages you, listen to her.

Listen to your mama!

I wrote you children a letter to read when I die. It is called, "I Died". You know about it. I try to update it every year. This year, I wrote one to your mama as well.

I am going to copy and paste the end of my letter to her. You will see why I tell you to listen to your mama.

"I have told you many times that any good in my life has come from Jesus and from God through YOU. I was just brainstorming, and these are some of the things that you have taught me through example, conversations and study. I don't really need to expand on them. I just want you to know that these things are in my life because of you. You are reading this because I have died. I believe that my life mattered. I believe that my life counted. I believe that because of your love and influence, I was a good man. Here is how you molded and shaped me:

- The Bible is our only foundation to life.
- We need to pursue a passionate love for God.

- Fearless Faith means going all in every time.
- Love others as you love yourself.
- Live a Holy Spirit filled life.
- Seek to please God not others.
- Live life with eternity in mind.
- Make decisions with long term in mind, not short term.
- Share Jesus....a lot.
- Family first.
- Forgive constantly
- Encourage daily.
- Give generously.
- Learn from everyone.
- Evaluate life by fruit not works.
- Compare with who you could be, not with others.
- Be 'all there' wherever and whenever 'there' is.
- Be a servant.
- Chase after wisdom.
- Make good plans but hold them loosely.
- Set big goals with little steps.
- Enjoy life and laugh a lot.
- Work hard all the time.
- Life is too short to....
- Touch others on their heart level.
- Marriage 1st, kids second.
- Try something new.
- Change what you can to reach people for Jesus, but never compromise essentials.
- There are not many essentials.
- I believe that I am right, but I might be wrong.
- Humility wins."

Notice how this book contains so many of her lessons to me. She is the Jedi and I am the Padawan. Your mama has your best interest in mind, the Holy Spirit filling her heart, and faith driven wisdom to share. She has life experience. Listen to your mama!

Your mama is the wisest and Godliest person you will meet. Listen to your mama.

GLORIFY GOD.

Go back to the Holman Family Creed as we close this book.

No Whiner Babies.
Apply The Stupid Rule.
Don't Be A Jerk.
Honor Christ In All You Do.
Be Kind To Everyone.
Always Tell The Truth.
Forgive Instantly.
Believe The Bible.

Look at number 4. Honor Christ in all you do.

I am going to end this book to you with one of the early chapters in my other book on discipleship. I think it is well written and expresses my heart to you.

"Put it on a bumper sticker." That is what I was told by a mission committee I was meeting with to gain support for our ministry. The man that said it had asked me about our ministry and I was rambling on about all we were doing and how we were doing it. He wanted me to give him the core essence and nothing more. He rephrased it by saying, "What is your ministry Tweet?"

So, with discipleship, what is the tweet? What is on your discipleship bumper sticker? What is the one core thing that makes one a disciple?

If there were any one thing by which to define, defend and/or describe the successful Christian life I think it would be this one. I believe if we can teach ourselves to do this one thing, it will change our lives. If we would learn to ask ourselves this question, and answer it honestly, then we will not only be on the road to victory, but we will also live in victory. This question applies to every situation. It is useful in every relationship. It redeems every moment.

We find it all throughout the Bible. It is so important it is usually the first question-and-answer part of catechisms. For example, the famous Westminster Shorter Catechism begins with the question we need to ask ourselves as the answer.

The question is, "What is the chief end of man?". This is asking us to define success. Why is it we are even in existence? The answer given in the catechism is to glorify God and to enjoy Him forever. Here is how I phrase the question for my life and what I try to teach others to ask themselves.

"How can I bring God glory in this moment?"

"Are my thoughts glorifying God?"

"Will the words I want to say bring God honor?"

"What action can I do that will cause God to receive glory?"

Here is a driving verse. Look at it and think about what it is saying to us.

Whether, then, you eat or drink or whatever you do, do all to the glory of God. (1 Corinthians 10:31)

God gets the glory. Period. I am to think, speak, and act in such a manner that I glorify Him. Romans 3:23 sums up the sinful condition of man as 'fallen short of the glory of God'. God summarized sin by saying it was us not glorifying Him. If you contemplate the depth of this one verse, it will transform you. God says we should seek to glorify Him in every part of our lives, and even the mundane task of taking a drink of water can be and should be done for His glory. Over 500 times in the Bible, God uses the word 'glory' or one of its synonyms. We are to glorify God.

For you have been bought with a price: therefore glorify God in your body. (1 Corinthians 6:20)

If whatever you are doing involves your body, then it should be done for the glory of God. This means thinking, since it involves your brain and your mind, should glorify God. Your words, since they engage your physical body, should glorify God. Your actions, because it uses your body, should glorify God.

The successful disciple is someone who follows Jesus and does what He tells them to do in order to glorify God. A successful disciple is someone who seeks to glorify God in every aspect of their life at every moment of their life. When your desire and your efforts are to glorify God in your thoughts, words, attitudes, actions, relationships, roles and accomplishments, then you are being successful in every way.

Go back to the life-defining moment of the death of my Son. His sudden death at 29 years of age rocked my world. My theology took a hit. My emotions were all over the board. My heart was and still is shattered by his loss.

As I was processing his death and preparing the message, I would give at his funeral, my mind was so full of questions. Let me share with you what I wrote in my journal and in my funeral message.

If we ask the wrong question, we will always end up at the wrong answer. We have to focus on the correct question. When an unexpected and tragic death hits you, the first question you ask again and again is this: Why did this happen? That question is a terrible question. The reason it is not a good question is because there is no answer that will help you. I heard so many platitudes in the weeks and months of his death. Most of them made me want to throw up because they were meaningless chatter. One phrase thrown out over and over is, "God has a purpose in this." It is also phrased in a guess what God's purpose is such as "I just know someone will come to Christ because of Seth's death."

The problem is that I know God has an infinite number of resources at His disposal. He did not have to kill my son to accomplish some little detail in His grand scheme of the universe. If He wanted one of my son's friends to come to Christ, then He could have used a friend sharing the gospel, a tract, a radio program, a childhood memory, a Bible verse, or a friend at work. You name it. He did not have to kill Seth to bring life to someone. When a parent loses a child, I promise you no reason will make them say, "Okay God, I understand. It is cool. Do You want to take another of my kids since it makes so much sense?"

Asking why serves no purpose except to leave you with emptiness and/or an anger or resentment at God. Asking why causes you to fill up the emptiness of no sufficient answer with bitterness. The devil gets you to ask why to cause you to question the love and/or power of God. Since there is no reason for this to have HAD to have happened, why did God let it? God must not love me. These attacks on God come from the poor question, "Why".

Another set of questions are in the 'What Now' category. These are task-oriented things that have to be done in order to have the funeral and all the details around a death. These questions do not help you deal with the crisis. They help you manage tasks the crisis created. These are not good or bad, they just are necessary.

The best question to ask in a time like this is: "How can I respond to this horrible tragedy in a way that will bring glory to God?" We need to move beyond what has happened and seek avenues on how to glorify God after it has happened. I do not want to be an embittered parent who has lost a child. I want to be a grieving father pointing others to the glory of God.

That is the reason I wrote the book "How Could My Son Be Dead?". I hoped people could see how we continue(d) to plod through the worst day/month/year of our life with a sincere desire to Glorify our Father.

I was/am grieving. I want my grief to bring Him glory.

I am broken by his death. I want my broken and shattered heart to reflect Him. I want my children to see God is worthy, and God is good even when life truly stinks. My life is not about my plans succeeding. My life is to be about the glory of God. My son dies, and God is still worthy of Glory. My heart breaks, and God is still worthy of Glory. His death is horrible. God is still worthy of Glory.

Life is not about getting the 'How To' checklists all finished so you can be super productive. It is not about understanding the deep and profound reasoning behind various philosophical discussions. Life is about the glory of God.

In our marriage workshops, we often teach on conflict and how to manage it. The first principle we explain is we are to glorify God. This conflict and how I respond to it is to glorify God. When my wife disagrees with me, the thoughts that go through my mind should be taken captive and brought into the obedience of Christ so the very thoughts I have about her, the event, the conflict and my answer should glorify Him. My words, both what I say and how I say them, in the very heated moment of the conflict itself, should be a balm to Christ and honor Him. My actions toward the conflict, the cause of the conflict and my wife and/or anyone else in the conflict should minister grace and love to the glory of God.

What would happen to your marriage if you asked these simple questions both proactively and in response to others?

"How can I bring God glory in this moment?"

"Are my thoughts glorifying God?"

"Will the words I want to say bring God honor?"

"What action can I do that will cause God to receive glory?"

What would happen in your parenting, and in the relationships you have with your children, if you examined your role as a parent considering these questions? Imagine you are encouraging your child, or you are disciplining them for their behavior and as you did it, these questions went through your mind:

"How can I bring God glory in this moment?"

"Are my thoughts glorifying God?"

"Will the words I want to say bring God honor?"

"What action can I do that will cause God to receive glory?"

List every role and relationship you have. You are a parent, child, sibling, cousin, friend, church member, employee, employer, co-worker, neighbor, citizen, etc. Now, in every one of those roles and relationships, what would happen if you asked those questions?

Go back to that verse.

"Whether, then, you eat or drink or whatever you do, do all to the glory of God." (1 Corinthians 10:31)

The first part of being a true follower of Christ is to realize as you are following Him, you are also pointing to Him. When people look at you and your life, they should see Christ being magnified.

The very first and the core component of real discipleship is learning in this moment every fiber of my being exists to glorify my Father Who is in heaven. Remember, the focus of being a disciple and of being a disciple maker is the Presence and Person of Jesus Christ. He is here and worthy of being glorified right now, and it is always right now.

Those words in my other book sum up my heart. Glorify Jesus.

My child, I share this book and our time learning it together in love. I am proud of you. I love you. I desire the best for you. I believe if you apply the principles in this book, your life will bless others.

So, my last words to you, "Before You Go": Love God. Glorify Him.

Made in the USA
Middletown, DE
20 March 2021